THE SPEECH I TEACH:
PUBLIC SPEAKING
FOR TODAY'S STUDENTS

MICHELLE DESELLE Ph.D.

Kendall Hunt
publishing company

D1621537

Kendall Hunt
publishing company

www.kendallhunt.com
Send all inquiries to:
4050 Westmark Drive
Dubuque, IA 52004-1840

Copyright © 2017 by Kendall Hunt Publishing Company

ISBN 978-1-5249-1123-2

Published in the United States of America

This textbook is dedicated to the people that cause me to love what I do . . . my students. And to the three that endearingly call me mother duck, Terry, Jay, and Sydney; I know pure love because of you. To Lionel, you have taken the very best care of me through every page, readings, and days I felt it impossible to do, no one can compare.

Give me what is owed, "knowledge" and I will increase its worth by imparting it into the minds of eager students.

Michelle DeSelle

Table of Contents

Part 1   **The Communication Process**   **1**

Chapter 1   Jump-Starting the Communication Process   3

Chapter 2   Public Speaking   23

Chapter 3   The Speech and How It All Comes Together   35

Chapter 4   Narrowing Your Topic and Acquiring Supporting Material   49

Part 2   **Developing Your Speech**   **57**

Chapter 5   The People in the Seats—Audience Analysis   59

Chapter 6   Verbal Communication   69

Chapter 7   Nonverbal Communication   83

Part 3   **Interpersonal Communication and Small Group**   **99**

Chapter 8   Interpersonal Relationships and Conflict   101

Chapter 9   Small Group Communication   115

Part 4   **How Public Speaking is Used**   **129**

Chapter 10   Teach Me Something—Speaking to Inform   131

Chapter 11   All We Do Is Argue—Speaking to Persuade   147

Chapter 12   Being Career Ready   157

Appendix   **163**

To the Instructor

I want each of you to wake up every day knowing that the life of practically every human being you encounter has been touched by or enhanced by someone of your profession. You are finely woven into the fabric that holds this Universe together. Every doctor, scientist, lawyer, politician, business person, or professor has been inoculated by the knowledge that you so graciously impart. Each of you too will attribute your success to an admired instructor as well, I know I do.

I wrote *The Speech I Teach: Public Speaking for Todays Student* because I felt the need to give students exactly what they needed to grasp and retain the information long term. The text also includes speeches written by top-performing public-speaking students. By introducing strategies and concepts that are memorable and effective, students will conceptualize techniques learned far beyond the assignment deadline and semesters end.

Knowing that effective public speaking is strategic, and involves an understanding of the rules that govern when to speak and where communication occurs, I found it absolutely necessary to foster approaches that would cater to the way students learn as opposed to bombarding the text with inflated theories and highfalutin research. Much of which students cannot cover in a four and a half month semester, meanwhile the textbooks become overwhelming, taxing, and boring. My take is, that the majority of textbooks are not written for students for whom they are intended but, however, are written by scholars for other scholars. And for this pitiful need to impress another scholar, our students are left to suffer painstaking attempts at reading unnecessarily long chapters which could have been explained in 10 pages but were drawn out into 30. Too often textbooks appear to be written by scholars with very flat affect as the text reads as such, with lack of emotional expression.

The experience of learning should be an enjoyable one. The key elements of critical thinking, strategic planning, and analytical skills are emphasized throughout this text. The student is of the utmost importance, therefore, my efforts are to equip them with the necessary skills and knowledge to prepare them to make skillful and intelligent communication choices.

My efforts are also to share enjoyable ways that instructors may utilize to make the learning environment effective and memorable for students. Below are tried and true techniques that work well for my students and aid in a pleasant and fun learning atmosphere.

Intro Speech

First day of class icebreaker! It is totally funny and unexpected for the whole class. After you take attendance, go to the board and write: Name, Major, Hobbies, Interest, and What you intend to get from the course. Tell your class to look it over, write it down if they need to, and in a few minutes go erase it and inform them that "today you will give your first speech of the semester, starting with the first person on the attendance record. You have two minutes, you cannot use any notes and it is worth 50 points. The class erupts with shock, laughter and "you can't be serious!" This is great because every student will keep looking at the blank board as though the list will reappear when they forget what comes next; this is when the classroom of strangers comes to their rescue to assist by whispering the next steps. This builds alliances, comradery, and they are knowing who their audience is, which prepares them for future speech assignments without feelings of heightened anxiety one might have in the presence of total strangers.

© Monkey Business Images/Shutterstock.com

The "Tee" That's Me

This activity is a real gem, students love it! I use this to serve as an audience analysis. I advise students to wear a special or favorite tee shirt that tells the class (their audience) unique facts about them. Sometimes it is the tee from their favorite concert, blood drive, or cause. This activity builds confidence, lessens anxiety, and also forms relationships among students. The familiarity it forms takes away that feeling of 25 strangers staring at me during speech day away. Students are captive audiences and getting demographics as one would for an off-campus speaking event is something altogether different. The commonality is they are all students in the same speech class, the "tee that's me" gets students sharing really great things about who they are, even answering class questions.

© NadinaS/Shutterstock.com

I'm the Instructor Now

This exercise is one of my favorite, I select a set of two students at a time to actually conduct the lecture for about five minutes, using my clicker and PowerPoint slides. I have them introduce themselves to the class example: "hello I'm Professor Britton" and "I am Professor Foster" and I serve as their trusty sidekick assistant (to assist if they get stumped). This is fun because it never fails that they will mimic my teaching style and the entire class gets a kick out of it.

But this prepares students in several ways: (1) they become comfortable in front of an audience; (2) it builds confidence and technique; (3) they get to actually multi-task using verbal and nonverbal communication skills, while answering audience questions; (4) they learn how to adapt to their audience before and during their lecture. Once they are done, select two more, students enjoy this experience immensely, many times requesting that I repeat it. This activity serves to increase their public speaking skills and build their confidence level.

Act It Out

This is done during the time we are preparing for persuasive speeches, when teaching the students about Aristotle's primary means of persuasion. I give several different scenarios and have them act them out having to use ethos, logos, and pathos to build effective persuasion. For example, I used two students, and the scenario was, one student needed to borrow the car of the other student to go home for a family emergency. The student had to incorporate each means of persuasion to try and reach the goal of obtaining the use of the other's car.

It is amazing to observe the measure students will employ to convince the other. I encourage instructors to take an active role in at least one of the scenarios, it is something students will appreciate and enjoy. This allows them to grasp the concepts involved in persuasive arguments and serves to build positive rapports with one another.

My Anxiety Has a Name

Indeed, it may sound bizarre but my students confirm that it is quite helpful. Now, this technique is something that I have used for many years but never intended to reveal it publicly as I thrive on being considered a "sane" individual; however, when I constantly witnessed my students struggle with anxiety issues in my public speaking classes, I knew I had to "take one for the team."

My anxiety's name is "Chanel." I do not consider my anxiety a boogie man or something negative. Anxiety is something that even the veteran public speaker experiences; it is not just reserved for the novice speaker. This is how it works: my anxiety "Chanel" will accompany me to the podium and will remain until just after I make eye contact with a pleasant face and give them a smile and render my credibility statement, I can feel my anxiety dissipate, then she leaves and disappears, she does not wait in the audience to hook back up with me afterwards either. She is gone until I need her for the next speech. Yes, "need" her; anxiety can serve to enhance your speaking ability if you will use it effectively. You know you have a job to do, and failing your audience is not an option, remember they are your first priority, it's not about "you" so allow your anxiety to help you present your topic, never allow it to diminish your speaking ability. Speaking and anxiety go hand in hand for many, very few admit to not having anxiety when speaking, so embrace it, it'll always accompany you so give it a name, respect it, and keep speaking.

I am indeed honored for the opportunity to offer this text; it is fun, relatable, audience focused, and 100 percent written with the student and instructor in mind. Keep speaking, I want to hear you.

Michelle DeSelle

PART 1

The Communication Process

Chapter 1

Jump-Starting the Communication Process

Learning Objectives

Exploration in this chapter will allow students to discover:

1.1. Defining What Communication Is
1.2. What Definitions Significantly Impact the Communication Process
1.3. Understand the Benefits and Pitfalls of Varying Communication Channels
1.4. Difference between the Linear, Interaction, and Transactional Models of Communication
1.5. The Elements of the Transaction Communication Model

© g-stockstudio/Shutterstock.com

1.1 Defining Communication

There is not an area of one's life that communication is not essential. The methods in which we communicate with those around us determine the level of success in our relationships. Whether the relationship is of a personal nature or professional, we have all certainly had moments when we lacked effective communication skills. This text has been designed to investigate in depth the various communication pitfalls that arise in our personal and professional lives and to teach the basic concepts to overcome them. The principles taught in this text will prepare you in whatever career path that you choose as well as strengthen one's personal relationships if they are properly applied. The chapters will summarize communication skills that you should have no reservations implementing to resolve issues and increase your communication capabilities at home and in the workplace.

We communicate on a daily basis; however, we may not think it important to define what the concept of communication is. To define such will give insight into how complicated and challenging the process of communication can be. According to Merriam-Webster's Collegiate Dictionary, eleventh edition, the word "communicate" is the act or process of using words, sounds, signs, or behaviors to express or exchange information or to express your ideas, thoughts, feelings, etc., to someone else. As we continue the study of communication, we learn that there is increasingly more room for progress and development, knowing this we will build on the definition set forth in this text and define *communication* as the exchange of thoughts, messages, or information, as by speech, signals, writing, or behavior. Anchored in this definition are numerous terms that significantly impact the communication process— *the exchange of thoughts*, *messages*, and *information*, by way of *speech*, *signals*, *writing*, and *behavior*. Let's jump-start the communication process by looking at each of these in greater detail.

1.2 Definitions That Impact the Communication Process

Communication, the Exchange of Thoughts, Messages, and Information

It is widely understood that when one communicates they will use various concepts in order to achieve the goal of sending and receiving messages being it through verbal or nonverbal means. The process of communication is continuous and ever evolving. Communication does not begin when you open your mouth to speak neither ends when you finish speaking. With this in mind, the process begins before you ever utter a word, taking into account your experience with the other person, their gender, culture, and overall frame of reference. The process may very well not involve the act of "speaking" at all but could greatly involve one's nonverbal communication, and the effects thereof may have lasting impacts well after the interchange has taken place. Often times the words spoken or actions of others continue to make an impact on one's feelings and actions.

When communication is defined as an *exchange* it is understood that one is giving up something for the equivalent in return. Exchanging symbols between communicators as in words, nonverbal concepts, and vocals create meaning. When exchanging thoughts, messages and information both parties are responsible for the outcome of the interaction and both are affected by it.

For communication to be successful, it is never solely about one individual doing something well; it is always due to both parties contributing to a satisfactory outcome. Moreover, when communication is unsuccessful, that, too, is the responsibility of both parties and both are affected by its failure. For example, when you and your lab partner exchange information and ideas on the treatment of the zika virus, you simultaneously affect each other's knowledge and perception of one another as well as the entire situation. You will also begin to analyze your own competence as individuals and human beings. How great it is to recognize the power each of us has to enhance the lives of others merely by the way we elect to communicate with them.

Communication: Effectively Creating Messages

When we think of messages it is a known fact that it is transmitted in many ways, but what is a *message* actually? Is it something spoken, written, or is it something that is done? Perhaps it is all of the above; *message* is defined according to Merriam-Webster as a communication in writing, in speech, or by signal. Now, allow me to teach you something as we explore the *written message*; In 1922, Emily Post lamented, "the art of general letter-writing in the present day is shrinking until the letter threatens to become a telegram, a telephone message, a post-card . . ." We can only imagine what she would think of email, instant messenger, and the abbreviated text messages of today. Long gone is the anticipation of receiving a hand written letter in the mail from a close friend, relative, or lover.

The intimate connection of the written message has been swallowed up by the age of technology in which we live, rare is the romantic card that one will cherish because it holds a delicate mist of his or her fragrance or sealed by the press of longing lips painted of red. Certainly February is an appropriate time for letter writing to capture the art of the written message to be savored, tucked in a purse to be read over and over again . . . well not when you can just send a "Be my Valentine" text and a picture of flowers. Sadly enough, but the stack of bills and the now very rare Christmas card (of which many have saved from years past to set out at Christmas because they are not sent anymore either) are the only thing one can expect in the mailbox.

It is highly important that the written message not be abandoned; studies show that there are many physical and mental benefits to this long-standing cultural practice. (Hall 2015) states that writing by hand can improve learning abilities to foster a more positive outlook on life; and when it comes to writing as a form of communication between two people, namely letters and postcards, the impact of such messages last far longer than any alternative version offered in our high-tech world.

More than likely, the majority of you reading this text were born in the age of technology thus the art of the handwritten letter as a form of communication is absolutely foreign and you may find that you have little use of it. However, the benefits of such an art are universal and we will now enlighten you of the various positive effects of written communication. Perhaps this new knowledge will inspire you to adopt this cultural practice as a part of how you communicate going forward.

Learning Benefits of Handwritten Communication

The internet, and the broad sea of electronic devices, has revolutionized the communications world with its worldwide broadcasting capabilities like nothing else ever has. Our way of communicating in past years involved extensive interpersonal interactions, which were direct face-to-face exchanges but this has changed drastically in the past 21 years as have the basic common core standards adopted in most states of "writing" taught to youth in early childhood development programs.

According to many educators, teaching students' handwriting matters very little, the focus is mainly on Kindergarten (German for "children's garden") and first graders being taught to write legibly, thereafter the primary goal is proficiency of the keyboard. Reading, Writing, and Arithmetic . . . were the chant taught in Elementary schools before internet and computers were introduced to early childhood learners. Youngsters were drilled each day to master these core subjects, every assignment was handwritten and evaluated for accuracy of spelling and if your letters met the correct form when writing them. Imagine attending school K–12 never using a computer, no cutting or pasting information, or having internet for research, this was just the case in the 1980s, not that long ago.

It is less difficult to lose this art form of communication if it was a regular part of your curriculum; however, when it is not, the student has been greatly deprived of necessary knowledge that will be needed personally as well as professionally.

The benefits to this written communication we speak of are vast and long lasting, the learning components and others are as follows.

Written Commination Ignites Creativity

Exploring the learning aspect of the handwritten message increases one's mental sharpness and creativity; taking out your pen and paper you utilize your motor, visual, and cognitive brain processes in a manner that differs significantly than when technology in incorporated to assist us. The process requires a bit more effort of us, it is more labor intensive, requiring you to connect the mind with the hand and slow down with each word written, thus being just what is needed to trigger those creative juices.

Written Communication Promotes Academic Success

The benefits of gripping and moving a pen or pencil go far beyond communication. Emerging research shows that handwriting skill increases brain activity and hone motor skills as mentioned above, it can also promote one's academic success in ways that keyboarding cannot. Students learn to read at an accelerated rate when they learn to write by hand and are then able to generate more ideas and retain information.

Two psychologists, Pam A. Mueller of Princeton and Daniel M. Oppenheimer of the University of California, Los Angeles, have reported that in both laboratory settings and real-world classrooms, students learn better when they take notes by hand than when they type on a keyboard. Contrary to earlier studies attributing the difference to the distracting effects of computers, the new research suggests that writing by hand allows the student to process a lecture's contents and reframe it—a process of reflection and manipulation that can lead to better understanding and memory encoding. (*Now you should really understand why I insist on "no computers in class for note taking."*) Berninger (2014) goes so far as to suggest that cursive writing may train self-control ability in a way that other modes of writing do not, and some researchers argue that it may even be a path to treating dyslexia.

Written Communication Creates Cherished Memories

Whether you are keeping in touch with family, kindling a romance, or cultivating a new relationship writing a letter or sending a postcard is a sentiment that will forever be remembered and cherished.

The handwritten note accompanying the care package of baked goods, cash, and toiletries sent to the college freshman will serve as a reminder that they are loved, missed, and will be just fine in their new surroundings. Moreover, it assures them that they are not alone and family is there for them and is confident in their abilities to do well.

Love letters kept in a shoebox of a lover deployed will be read many times over to console one in a time of longing and loneliness. Moments are relived, smiles will resurface and you will be constantly reminded of your commitment and why you fell in love with them in the first place.

The postcard sent to that new friend you met while traveling abroad ensures that they've not been forgotten, and that the instant connection that was so great between the two of you causing you to laugh uncontrollably at each other's stories will have the promise of flourishing into a lasting friendship that will explore the many things you discovered the both of you had in common.

Written Communication: Make Every Word Count

When taking the time to send a handwritten letter to someone, you enter into a great deal of thought of what to say and how to say it. For example; when sending a postcard you have very limited space in which to write, therefore there is no room for error unlike with an email, text message, or Facebook message; you only get that one chance when writing a handwritten message, so make every word count, do not allow your great words of expression to be wasted. You and you alone have the ability to encourage, inspire, and to comfort with your words . . . so write them and make them count.

Written Communication: It Is Timeless

"More than kisses, letters mingle souls."

— John Donne

It is true, now allow me to teach you how, when your words are written on stationary and mailed or given to that special person they become immortal, they become a part of a timeline, one's history, a keepsake, a reminder of love and or forgiveness. Long after you, the sender, and the receiver, have experienced the offerings of a written letter and are gone, the letter remains to be read, preserved, and appreciated. Some of the most historic letters are procured and displayed in museums for the entire world to enjoy. The written word protects memories of lives lived in a unique way; unlike technological communication, letters are personal, tangible, and real in every sense of the word, hence they are Timeless.

Written Communication Requires Undivided Attention

For one to take on the joy of handwriting, it requires you to summons all of your senses to participate, and the usual engagement of multitasking must take a backseat. To write meaningfully and thoughtfully, we must be focused on the moment, dismissing all side conversations and to-do lists so that you are better able to coherently convey your message to the receiver of your letter. Your undivided attention will be noticed when the receiver reads your words and is then able to feel their meaning, and display the smile you intended to bring to them.

Written Communication Requires One to Unplug

In the world we live in it seems impossible to manage without our technology, be it a laptop, cell phone, or IPad. We are walking gadget-holders and -scrollers! Undoubtedly we could all use a bit of screen-free time, so sit and pick up a pen and write a line or two to that special someone. Indeed it may confuse your thumbs when they are not scrolling Facebook or texting a friend needing your immediate attention. For that time you will need to unplug and live in the present to compose a heartfelt sentiment that will remain special because it was in your written words.

Written Communications Show You Care

Our lives are made up of people who mean a lot to us: family, friends, or significant others. We are prone to wanting them to know we care for them, and we exhibit this in many ways. Sending a "just because" email is a big deal for special someones but imagine taking the time to actually write that "just because" letter, purchase a stamp, mail it, and wait the days it may take to get to the receiver. Once, the receiver gets that letter, they are joyful, smiling, and knows they are truly cared for, that says it all.

As stated earlier there are many benefits to handwritten communication and it is the author's hope that you will partake in this cultural tradition on your own. To get you started on page eight (8) of your text, there is a page titled *"just because"* in your text, you are to tear it out, write a letter to a person of your choosing and give it or mail it and report how it made you feel and the response of the receiver. You may make additional copies if you wish.

You've spoken sweetly to me, you've held me close, yet when the sound of your voice is faint and your touch out of reach it is your letters that embrace me until we meet again.

— Author's own

Just Because

Dear _____

_____

_____

_____

_____

_____

_____

_____

_____

_____

_____

_____

_____

_____

_____

_____

_____

_____

_____

Sincerely, _____

1.3 Benefits and Pitfalls of Varying Communication Channels

Communication: Messages through Speech

Who among you has something to say? (Are those crickets I hear?) Why communicate through speech when you have email, twitter, Facebook and the "Mother" of them all text messaging? These forms of technology (until updated) will always play significant roles in our society, in like manner, so shall speech as a form of communication be, if not more significant. There are various reasons why the above-mentioned forms of electronic communication are preferred by its users and we are going to teach you something about the pros and cons of each one as well as discuss the benefits of speaking . . . yes the great act of face-to-face contact.

Communicating through Email: Pros and Cons

Emailing is a form of communicating that you will see most used in the workplace, and has minimal use by millennials.

One main reason we can argue is that it is free, well last I checked no one was running a meter during face-to-face interaction either, tallying up how many words you used to explain the details of a scheduled meeting and giving you an invoice. However, we can all agree that there are some people of whom we'd wish to pay to get out of our faces.

© Adisorn Saovadee/Shutterstock.com

It Is Fast

You have a message to be sent, it is done in a matter of seconds, but what if that message was sent in the heat of the moment and after you have had a chance to process what you have said, you have regrets and second thoughts about the content in that email. Well one thing about communication . . . spoken or electronic once it is sent it is irreversible, you cannot get it back. Herein lies the beginning of your problems, a damaged personal relationship or a severed professional one that will lead to you being escorted out with a small box bearing the contents of an office or cubicle. Weigh it, cool your jets walk a few steps and talk it over face to face.

© Milles Studio/Shutterstock.com

Information at Your Fingertips

Who doesn't need a little convenience every now and then, indeed emailing gives us the advantage of storing data online as opposed to the large file cabinets and shelves of yesteryear, allowing you to access data quicker if you took the time to learn to use email in this way. Just remember this, more than one's intellect grows while just sitting and clicking, so getting up walking down the hall to the records room may be just what you need to get the blood flowing and boost up the calories you desire to burn for the day.

Creativity is best when it flows through a vessel of good health.

— Authors own

It Is Green

Now the advantages and disadvantages of email are crystal clear here. It is in fact good for the planet; however, computers themselves aren't green but email does offset the damage by reducing the environmental cost of face to face contact. That is, fuel for transportation, quality of air, water, and land around the world.

© rvlsoft/Shutterstock.com

Global Touch

Email keeps you in touch personally and professionally around the globe. You are able to access it anywhere at any time. Traveling abroad? You can email yourself your passport number, boarding pass, and traveler's insurance.

Email is a good and productive tool if used well, although there is a flip side, and they are as follows.

Disadvantages of Email

Information Overload

I make it a habit (unless my students have really pushed the envelope) to keep my correspondence to them brief and to the point, giving them the what, when, and how. Too often too many people send too much information and to cover their butt's they cite "Need to Know" in the subject box as justification, and it turns out to be the content that you are not interested in, or they are on yet another get-rich-quick scheme and they need to recruit people for their up line, or simply just a huge waste of your time.

© verbaska/Shutterstock.com

Misunderstandings

This is something that is so easy to happen when emailing family, friends, or co-workers. Many times the sender doesn't take the time to check what is typed before sending, and there is a huge amount of time wasted trying on either clarifying what you meant or even worse acting on misinterpretations of messages.

Eats Up Time

It is so common for us to see our email and feel obligated to reply, which will result in our over-replying in many

© wavebreakmedia/Shutterstock.com

cases causing it to eat up valuable time needed for more pressing and important task. It is good practice to check your inbox once or twice a day, quickly reply to those matters of high importance (work related), then off to a productive day.

Too Long

What is too long when it comes to email? Well as stated earlier email is most widely used in the workplace, therefore it is sent to co-workers, staff, and colleagues who are extremely busy without a lot of time to sit and read; remember, your email should not pull the receiver into reading a novel, emails are suited for brevity . . . keep it short and sweet.

Now that you have been taught something about some of the pros and cons of email, let's discuss some about using Twitter as a form of communicating.

© Monkey Business Media/Shutterstock.com

Communication through Twitter: To Tweet or Not to Tweet

Twitter is a free social networking microblogging service that allows registered members to broadcast short posts called tweets. Members can also follow other user's tweets by using multiple platforms and devices. These broadcasts are limited to 140 characters due to the restraints of Twitter's Short Message Service (SMS) delivery system; because tweets can be delivered to followers in real time, they may seem like instant messages as well. Twitter's tweets are permanent and public: anyone can view them, even nonmembers.

Although users gush about the fact that Twitter's accessibility affords them the privilege of getting breaking news instantly, sharing ideas, gathering information, self-promote, promote others, as well as undeniable access to lawmakers and favorite celebrities, there are certainly pitfalls users should be mindful of.

© tanuha2001/Shutterstock.com

Pitfalls to Tweeting

All Eyes on Me!

You are on display; everybody is watching your every chirp, so you should be watchful of misuse. If not careful you can create a nightmare in the career department, employers use Twitter to screen out employees. A survey conducted by careerbuilder.com found that many employers use Twitter to reject potential employees whose Twitter profiles include provocative photos, evidence of drug use or drinking, negative posts about previous employers or co-workers, or comments that might be interpreted as racist, sexist, or ageist. Who could forget 2013's Justine Sacco scandal, in which the PR exec's last minute tweet before boarding a 12-hour flight got her fired before her plane had even landed: "Going to Africa. Hope I don't get AIDS. Just kidding. I'm white!" Whoa! You are what you Tweet!

It Drains Productivity

Excessively mining the feed for news that interest you, time taken to compose post, respond to others, reposting, and constant perusing—drains productivity. All that is evidence to employers that the habit is getting in the way of actual work being done. Reminder; it takes less than 140 characters to compose a pink slip!

Mind Your Self-Esteem

Great obsessions with what's going on in everyone else's life will ensure that you began to neglect what is going on in your own life right in front of you. Spending long periods on Twitter lurking to discover what celebs and others are doing, wearing, or whom they are dating can promote self-doubt, insecurity, and isolation. You will then begin to believe that others are more successful, privileged, happier, and overall better off than yourself. Obsess over your own self-esteem!

Trash Tweeting

It is ever so tempting to trash tweet when you are angry with someone, saying harsh insulting things about someone may make them look bad indeed but it can also backfire and make you look even worse. Moreover, in doing so it is certainly going to provoke the person on the receiving end and a war of words would begin and who knows their trash tweeting may be more damaging than yours could ever be. A case in point: rap artists Meek Mill and Drake's Summer 15 Twitter war over the ghostwriting accusations initiated by Mill provoked Drake to retaliate and then release tracks that caused Mill greater embarrassment. Fans chimed in with their tweeted opinions and radio disc jockeys had lengthy commentary on his inability to respond to Drake's clever responses as they came "back-to-back." So remember, use Twitter for its intended purpose because your tweeting may cause you a verbal beating.

Communication: Facebook

Facebook is a social networking website that makes it easy for you to connect and share with your family and friends online. Originally designed for college students, Facebook was created in 2004 by Mark Zuckerberg while he was enrolled at Harvard University. By 2006, anyone over the age of 13 with a valid email address could join Facebook. Today, Facebook is the world's largest social network, with more than 1 billion users worldwide.

© Rvlsoft/Shutterstock.com

One can ask the question, is Facebook good or bad? Well that certainly depends on who you are asking; many swear by the social networking site and some believe it is the devil. Whatever the opinion . . . good, bad, or indifferent, the ridiculed and crucified many times over popular networking site is here to stay. No decline in the use of Facebook in sight now or in the near future. There are various reason's people frequent the social networking site on a daily basis; some visit many times daily, every hour on the hour composing posts updating the world on meaningless things like pictures of what they are about to eat, to personal information like disputes in their relationships, to heartwarming stories of thoughtful garbage men being some little three-year-old girl's hero, and the list goes on and on. Let us now explore some of the *benefits* and alarming risk of using this omni-present social networking site.

Simple Enrollment

The process of setting up your profile is quite easy, set up is free, and all is needed is internet connection on any electronic device, even your cell phone, and you are well on your way. You will also enjoy the ease of use navigating throughout the site as it is uncluttered.

Sharing Is Caring, or Is It?

You decide who you share your statues, pictures, or check-ins with. You have the freedom of choosing if your page is private of public, sharing with discretion is important for safety purposes, accepting random friend request of unknowns to rack up numbers is a risky practice and should be avoided.

Positive Sharing

Facebook is where many share thoughts, ideas, and like interest with others across the globe. It is also where you may join fan pages and social groups.

Now that we have briefly addressed some of the benefits, let's discuss some of the alarming risks involved in using Facebook.

Is This Really You?

Things are not always as they appear; many profiles are fake as is much of the content people post about themselves and their lives. The networking site is a gathering place for unsavory characters with ill intentions, and unfortunately many youth could also be exposed to such.

Freedom of Expression?

As with Twitter, Facebook was designed for a particular purpose; however, its users have created their own reasons for this platform and use their freedom to express offensive and inappropriate content that appears on all of their friend's pages, many of which do not share the same thoughts or feelings, which leads to the next point . . .

Human Beings Can Be Mean!

When we hear cyberbullying, most of us automatically think of kids and teens; however, many adults are bullied on social networking sites as well. The campaign for cyberbullying does not make many concessions for the many adults who suffer and are in fear of their antagonist; many are bullied in social chat rooms, posts on social networking sites, or company email. Research shows that it is not taken seriously when reported to URL sites, they merely state that they are going to remove the person but many times it does not, it was even told by a person that was being bullied on a blog to "stop reading the blog if it was painful to read." Bendig (2014) states in an article she wrote for the Huffington Post that "in many cases bullying acts as a coping mechanism and a way to overcompensate for a lack of self-worth and perhaps is experiencing hardships in their lives." For many individuals social media has provided web-based courage, unlike in their real life whereas they may have been bullied themselves or cowards before, but what they do not realize is that even under the covering of the internet they still reveal strong signs of inadequacies and insecurities when they have a need to be malicious to others. There are not many forums that address this issue; however, an effort has been put forth to find a few and if help is needed to any reader of this text, feel free to use them, they are as follows.
www.Nobulling.com and bullingstatistics.com

"Hurting me still leaves a hurting you"

— Author's own

Do the pros outweigh the cons? It is difficult to say but you should take every necessary step to be mindful of how you use Facebook making every attempt to be professional, courteous, and think futuristic . . . some actions come back to bite you in the butt.

Communication: Text Messaging Can't Talk Right Now . . . Text Me

How many times have we seen this? Many have abandoned talking on the phone altogether and merely text instead. "If you need a prompt response text me." A text message is an electronic communication sent and received by cellular phone. Texting is also a proven way how communication gets misinterpreted. Often we read them and assume someone is angry or insensitive. This form of technology has caused many deaths as many choose to text while driving. Just as it has caused many ruined reputations due to sending content of an inappropriate sexual nature, i.e., sexting, not to mention the charges of child porn against students who were older spreading the content of their younger peers. However convenient this quick alternative to talking on the phone or face-to-face contact, there are many drawbacks to it as well.

© saswell/Shutterstock.com

Although amazing strides have been made in the realm of communication, there is still issues with communication being lost when not done face to face. Understanding that texts do not have a tone of voice, many will exert a tone themselves and misconstrue the message entirely, creating a recipe for disaster. It is important to know that someone's perception is not reality. From a text message, a person can imagine you doing something other than what you are, or might fail to understand what you are saying via text message.

We are a society that craves convenience and texting is one of those, but let's face it, it's one that wreaks havoc when it goes wrong. Face to face communications provides tones, expressions, and complete understanding of a message, but if texting has to be used, here are some suggestions that will assist in lessening the word wars.

Consider the Sender

Once that text is opened and read, reread it and think of the sender. Is it in their nature to say such things? Could they be in a hurry or in a compromising situation? Also, consider the type of relationship you have with the sender, friend, family, professional, or companion. Before, you react and send your replies, give yourself time to process, and if you must text, ask the sender for clarity . . . "Hello, got your text, could you please explain?" This method will give the sender an opportunity to recheck the message sent and realize an error or be able to give you a clearer explanation.

Keep Your Emotions in Check

When we react prematurely without getting a clear understanding, trouble is on the rise. Our goal should be to read text assertively and not emotionally. You should never allow your personal emotions to determine the meaning of the message. Remember, communication is irreversible: once it's out there you cannot get it back. Clarity is key! It will save you from the misery of arguments in the future.

Shots Fired!

Indeed that text rubbed you the wrong way! It is true that some text are meant to push your buttons, even still keep in mind to think rationally and calmly, heated text provokes heated responses and shots are fired to one up the other person and many times the shots result in threats being made, which is documented proof of which will hold up in a court of law. In which case, the Judge can shoot you some heavy fines or some lengthy time. It's just not worth it, reply to the person like so . . . "When you cool off perhaps we can talk about this over coffee." If hostile text persists, you can choose not to indulge; it is your phone after all.

Things Just Got Serious

Well, if that is the case then texting is the wrong source of communication. Never use texting to discuss matters of a serious nature, i.e., relationship issues, illnesses, finances, or the professor or co-worker you dislike. Issues of this nature should always take place during a one-on-one conversation where you have the privilege of exercising discretion, hearing the person's tone of voice, and seeing their facial expressions unlike the emotionless words of a text where misinterpretations are frequent, private issues are in writing, and people believe what they want. So if the topic is serious, use texting to set a time to "meet and take a seat!"

Much of what we have grown accustomed to technically or many of whom have been born into has become a huge part our everyday lives; hopefully now that you have learned about the sacred written and spoken forms of communication, you will be more apt to incorporate them more when communicating with others. Take time to unplug and engage one another with stimulating conversation instead of sending that emoji to express how you are feeling. Moreover, you should certainly have reason now to reevaluate your presence on social media sites, Twitter, Facebook, email, and text messaging are all useful if used in the manner in which they were intended; always remember to think first, respond out of good judgement not emotion. Remember . . . regrouping is far better than regretting!

Communication: The Exchange of Information

Our definition of *communication* includes the idea that when communication happens, the exchange of information takes place to express ourselves to one another. Knowing that the communication process can be complex, it also has a wide range of steps in order to take place. To effectively communicate we must examine the various models. *Models* are visual conceptualizations that explain the human communication process. Research shows that the very first model of communication was developed in 1949 by Claude Elwood Shannon and Warren Weaver for Bell Telephone Laboratories. Shannon was an American mathematician and the father of information theory, Weaver was also a mathematician as well as a scientist. Together these two scientists pioneered communication theories that has shaped the way humans communicate, the way scholars teach communication, also the way scientists continue to explore the ever-evolving field of communication. Let's find out more.

1.4 Difference between the Three Models of Communication

What distinctions exist between the linear, interactive, and transactional model of communication.

The three communication models give extensive insight into how the evolution of the communication process has changed the way we interact when sending and receiving messages—the linear model, the interactive model, and the transactional model. Each of these models has been improved by introducing elements of the communication process that are considered more accurate in what actually happens when we interact with one another.

Linear Models

We will first explore the Linear Model of Communication, also referred to as the action model. The linear model is a one-way transmission of messages beginning with the sender and ending with the receiver (Shannon and Weaver 1949). Shannon and Weaver distinctly designed this model with only three primary parts, which

Figure 1.1 Linear Model of Communication

Many Early Perspectives were Linear

*One way—from Sender to Receiver

ideally mirrors radio and telephone technologies. The linear model has a sender who only speaks but does not listen, a listener who only hears but does not respond. The three parts are *sender*, *channel*, and *receiver*. We will go further in-depth of each part later in the text (see Figure 1.1). The *sender* encodes (verbal of nonverbal) a message as well as selects the *channel* (by which the said message is transmitted such as a cell phone) sends message to a *receiver* who decodes (interprets/ reconstructs) the message, many times in the presence of *noise* (internal or external distractions), which could be the absence of signals or just outright interference.

In this model you will notice that it is incomplete even considered flawed in that the element of feedback is not present thus the sender cannot be certain that the message was interpreted by receiver for the desired outcome, creating the inability to know if effective communication has occurred.

A more complete model has been illustrated by the *interaction model*, which includes the element of feedback; this model was introduced by Schramm (1965). His model saw the receiver or listener offering feedback to the sender or speaker. The sender or speaker of the message also listens to the feedback given by the receiver of listener. Both sender and receiver take turns to speak and listen to one another. Feedback is given verbally or nonverbally or in both ways; a breakdown of the process is presented in Figure 1.2. The interaction model has a *sender* who encodes (verbal or nonverbal) messages and selects a *channel* (cell phone, email etc.) to transmit the message to a *receiver* who decodes (interpret/reconstructs), who then provides *feedback* to the sender and the interaction is them mirrored by the sender until communication goals are met, all of which happens in the presence of *noise* (internal/external distractions). Notice that communication is better between the two if they have a *frame of reference* (individual perspectives) that overlaps.

Transactional models are a more recent, realistic, and complete representation of human communication. These models (introduced by Barnlund 1970) see communication as a transactional process—which means that both parties are equally responsible for creating meaning, they are both sender/receivers, not just a sender

Figure 1.2 Interaction Model

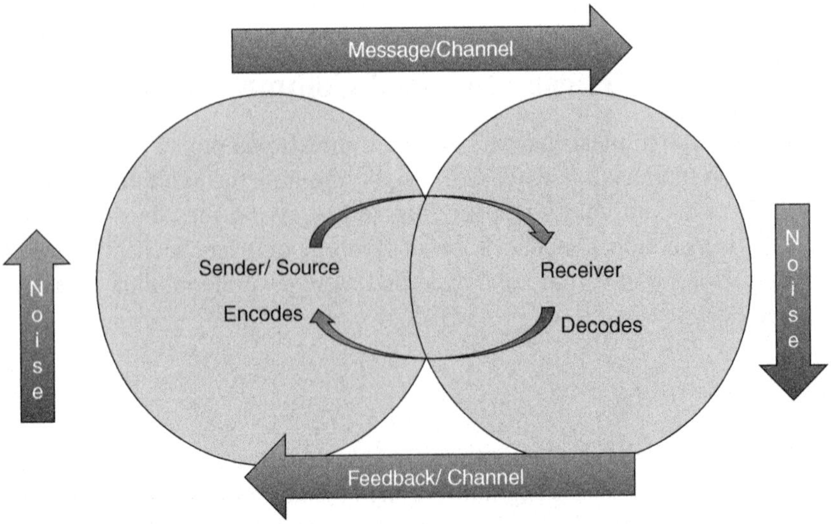

Message/Channel

Sender/ Source
Encodes

Receiver
Decodes

Noise

Noise

Feedback/ Channel

or a receiver. Both parties are then engaged in a transaction; therefore communication is simultaneous (see Figure 1.3). The *sender,* the initiator of the idea/message, *encodes* (puts the idea into spoken language) the message, then sends it through a *channel*; (medium through which the message travels), like oral communication (in-person, radio, television) or in written form (email, text message, letter), then to the *receiver*, the listener, who then *decodes* (translates or interprets) the sender's idea/message into something they can understand from their own *frame of reference* (personal perspective) and then sends feedback (the receiver's verbal or nonverbal responses) such as a shoulder shrug (nonverbal) indicating "I don't know," a nod (nonverbal) for understanding, or asking a question (verbal) for clarity. During the transactional process of communication, it is certainly not taking place without *noise* (internal/external distractions or interference) nor without *context* (where communication takes place). As you can see, the transaction model includes all elements of the previous models but also several new elements and ways to looking at and understanding our own way of communicating. Therefore, as we discuss the basic elements of communication, we will refer to the transactional model.

1.5 Elements of the Transaction Communication Model

Now that we have taken a peek into each of the communication models, we will now actually use the transaction model—the most recent and complete model—to recognize and discuss each element of the basic communication process; sender/receiver, message, channel encoding/decoding, feedback, noise, frame of reference, and context. While we attempt to teach you something about each element, make a conscious effort to recognize how each one applies to your everyday interaction while communicating with others, and where in the communication process problems may exist for you.

Sender/Receiver

There are two essential elements in every communication situation, the sender and the receiver. The sender is anyone who wishes to convey an idea or concept to others and the receiver is the person who responds to the idea or concept; however, it is from the transaction model where we will get a more detailed and accurate account of what truly goes on when people communicate with one another. As we saw in the linear model, the *sender* is the person who initiates the communication process and the *receiver* is the person in whom the message is directed toward. We then saw in the interaction model, that both parties send and receive but in a seemingly circular manner and feedback is introduced. The transactional model is a more dynamic model in that it enhances the way

Figure 1.3 Transaction Models

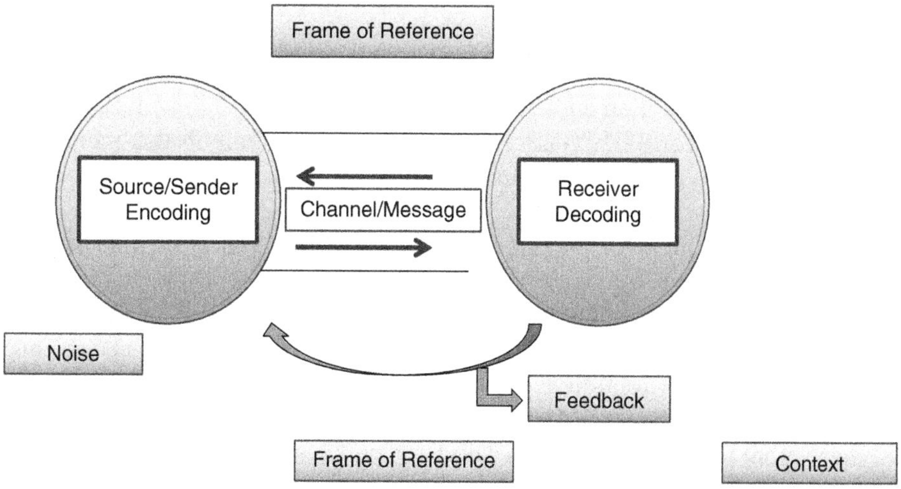

we view the sender and receiver by its illustration of communication as a *simultaneous* process. For example, when an employee explains to their supervisor that they are in need of a raise during a quarterly evaluation, the supervisor is actively listening, making eye contact, observing employee's actions, using nonverbal gestures while the employee stresses the fact that they have shown growth in leadership, project completion, and career development. All while the employee is monitoring the supervisor to ensure they understand the content of the message, whether the supervisor is for or against the request for his raise, or if extensive dialogue is needed to prove the request is merited. Both are engaged in the communication process whether verbal or nonverbal simultaneously; moreover, speakers are always going to attend to the reactions of audience members to gauge whether or not the message requires modification in order for desired effect to be achieved.

Message

The message is the feeling, idea, or thought that a communicator desires to convey to others. Simply put, it is the information you want to communicate; however, it goes much deeper than that, once that thought enters your mind you then begin to play out the situation mentally. Imagining the steps of the idea, considering who you will call, how they can relate and contribute to your idea. You may then start the process of writing out your thought to add visualization, which makes your idea take on the element of reality. It is then that the message itself is ready to be communicated with another person, but you also must consider this key factor that is overlooked while we are so involved with the tangibles; of what we say, how we are going to say it, even the method of delivery that we completely forget about the most powerful intangible—*listening*. There is no message to communicate if a listening ear does not cradle it and give it advancement. Never mind the act of getting someone's "attention" because "attention" is fleeting. The most effective communicators know that no matter how well thought out or brilliant the delivery of a message is, there is absolutely no guarantee of connection. Great communication connection comes through someone choosing to exercise *intentional listening*.

The sender of messages must understand that communication is not guaranteed; therefore it is essential to thoroughly analyze the audience and plan the message carefully as communication can be complex and difficult. Also, what we say is not always the way we convey our messages; although messages are usually sent intentionally, keep in mind that we are always communicating feelings or ideas whether we intend to or not. Simply put, communication is intentional and unintentional. Sitting in the back of the class with your head cradled in the palm of your hand (when you usually sit in the front actively participating in lectures) seemingly frustrated, sends a message that is loud and clear to others in the class. Even when you don't think you are sending a message or communicating, you most definitely are. You should know that the messages you send are not just verbal but nonverbal ones as well, also known as a *code* (hand gestures, facial, and vocal tones). Raising your eyebrow and giving the side eye to a comment a person just made may communicate your feelings that they are a dishonest snake louder that anything you could say with words.

Code

Each time you are in the presence of an audience, the message you convey involves three communication codes: verbal, nonverbal, and vocal. *Verbal codes* consist of language symbols that include written and spoken words. *Nonverbal codes* are codes of communication symbols that are not words, which encompasses bodily movement, facial expressions, gestures, eye contact (also referred to as visual codes) posture and personal appearance. *Vocal codes* include, volume, vocal quality, pitch, rate, and tone of voice. An effective communicator understands that these codes are highly important in the communication process; when we use verbal codes they are essential in imparting knowledge to others or conveying our own needs whereas the use of nonverbal codes (which coexist alongside verbal communication) can change one's perception, give off mixed signals, or positively reinforce verbal communication. It is the code that is closely monitored during interactions with others, as they are noting (visual and vocal cues) to see if your nonverbal codes are congruent with your verbal codes. For example, you have purchased a dress for a date you have planned later tonight; however, now you doubt your choice and asked your roommate's opinion, if she liked the dress you picked out. Your roommate responds, "oh sure I like it." Having said this with a smirk on her face and a sarcastic tone of voice, you would gather an accurate interpretation of insincerity from her nonverbal cues to what she really meant. Those cues certainly serve to reverse the meaning of the comment entirely. Research shows that when adults seek to understand the meaning of messages, they are more apt to rely on the voice and vocal cues than on spoken words (Archer & Akert, 1977, Burgoon & Hobbler, 2002). It is important as communicators that we not see the verbal code as the only important code and overlook the other two when speaking and sending messages. To truly be an effective speaker you must be able to send the same messages using all three codes.

Channel

Individuals wishing to send a message must next select a *channel*—a channel is the medium through which a message is transmitted to its intended audience, such as verbal or nonverbal, print or broadcast. If you choose to deliver a verbal message to someone, you may do so using spoken language, which can then be accomplished by using a cell phone as the channel or the face-to-face channel. Perhaps the verbal message is of a personal, business, or intimate nature and you desire to have a record of it, therefore you can choose to send your verbal message in writing using the channels of letters, text messages, e-mails, or social media. If the masses have to be informed of important situations involving our nation or community (public health crisis or government concerns for example) you may use the television or radio as the medium to convey a verbal message.

Be mindful of the channel you choose because each method has its own consequences if used improperly. For example, in 2006, Abercrombie & Fitch CEO Mike Jeffries gave an interview to Salon.com in which he stated that the retail chain's clothes were exclusively for thin, attractive, "cool kids." Also stating that "In every school there are the cool and popular kids, and then there are the not-so-cool kids," he says. "Candidly, we go after the cool kids. We go after the attractive all-American kid with a great attitude and a lot of friends. A lot of people don't belong (in our clothes), and they can't belong. Are we exclusionary? Absolutely. Those companies that are in trouble are trying to target everybody: young, old, fat, skinny." In 2013, a widely read Business Insider blog post breathed new life into the comments Jefferies gave and stirred up strong social media criticism from consumers, popular bloggers, social media, and influential individuals.

When choosing a channel, consider these important factors as well:

- Message Importance. Face-to-face channel is the most effective way to insure instant understanding, as both verbal and nonverbal codes are used simultaneously, this is certainly true the more important the message is.
- Relationship. Channel choice is crucial depending on the relationship one has with an individual: for a business associate you may select the e-mail channel opposed to a friend for whom you would select the text messaging or cell phone channel, and for family you would most often use face-to face channel and so on.
- Receiver needs and competence. Many receivers are affective decoders of e-mail and telephone messages; others prefer both the verbal and nonverbal codes found in face-to-face messages
- Feedback importance. If immediate feedback is needed, none is better than face-to-face; e-mail and telephone are fast if someone is available to check the e-mail or answer the phone; many times you hear "sorry, I haven't checked my email today" or "I was busy and unable to answer the phone."
- Cost. Email or text messages are more cost effective than long-distance calls or preparing for face-to-face interactions.
- Context. Where you are will determine the channel you choose to communicate with others; for instance, in an organized setting (conference, church, faculty meeting for example) you would select the channel that is more suitable to be mindful of being inappropriate, disrespectful, or disruptive.

Feedback

An equally important element of the communication process is *feedback*—the verbal and nonverbal responses to messages sent to a receiver or audience. In the action model the feedback element was not introduced, communication was one way and the interaction model feedback was said to be a circular process. However, in the transaction model both communicators are sending and receiving simultaneously, meaning both are encoding messages and decoding feedback at the same time. Feedback is essential because it is the only way we have of knowing our messages are received otherwise we can only guess and many times guessing causes much discord. When getting feedback through the face-to-face channel, you not only use your verbal code but your verbal and nonverbal codes thus having immediate answers to questions. This is because you have instant access to a person's facial expressions, tone of voice, and eye contact. Moreover, feedback allows you to correct encoding and decoding errors, one communicator may be good at encoding and decoding and the other may not be as skilled at it, which can lead to misunderstanding in the communication process as opposed to shared meaning. Ever heard these comments . . . "You have zero understanding" or "the more I teach you the dumber I get," some people have decoding difficulties and there are those who are just easier to communicate with than others. For instance, the teen that has to be given a directive repeatedly due to having trouble interpreting instructions, the best friend who frustrates you because they just can't understand basic logic, or the co-worker has issues interpreting simple instructions or the one who totally botch up when attempting to encode instructions thus making it impossible to follow them. Feedback is obviously needed.

Noise

The element of noise was added to the communication process very early on, *noise* is defined as any type of disruption that interferes with the transition or interpretation of information from the sender to the receiver. In general there are two categories of noise—external and internal. *External noise* refers to any distraction in your environment, such as loud sounds, or unusual movements causing you to be distracted. These noises make it hard to gather your thoughts as you speak to others or cause difficulty decoding messages you receive. *Internal noise* is anything that is happening within you that interferes with you sending or receiving messages effectively. Internal noise has two types you should know:

- *Psychological noise* refers to a person's internal preoccupations, prejudices, and other qualities that affect his ability to understand and communicate, distraction from within rather than outside the individual. If you are worried about the visit with your advisor after class about fulfilling all requirement for graduation, you are probably not going to able to focus well on your professor's lecture.
- *Physiological noise* is the physical or chemical functions of the body that compromises the effectiveness of communication. Examples are hunger, fatigue, headaches, pains, and physiological effects from medications that affect the way you feel.

Frame of Reference

In addition to the elements of the communication process we have just covered, there is another area where *frame of reference* differences affect the success of our communication—it is a complex set of assumptions and attitudes that we use to filter perceptions to create meaning. The frame can include beliefs, preferences, values, culture, and other ways in which we bias our understanding and judgment. As we move forward in this section, you may realize concepts that have caused you problems when communicating.

Communication and Beliefs

Belief can be defined as a state or habit of mind in which trust or confidence is placed in some person or thing. Beliefs are the foundation of which we build, we gather our beliefs from those around us from an early age, our beliefs serve as a baseline for what is or is not acceptable; moreover they mold our habits, patterns and behaviors and ways of thinking and being. They tell us what to trust what to fear, what to think, feel, say and do to belong, succeed, be happy, and avoid getting hurt. To help us know who we are, beliefs create our affiliations, what we like and who we want to associate with. Effective communicators will always be considerate and caring of others belief system and stay mindful not to offend, and be aware of receivers facial expressions and body language to know if they have miss stepped so that they may rectify the error by asking for their point of view or stop speaking on the matter at once.

Communication and Culture

Culture can be defined as the sum of attitudes, customs, and beliefs that distinguishes one group of people from another. Culture is transmitted, through language, material objects, ritual, institutions, and art, from one generation to the next. Among these groups are also co-cultures, which are smaller groups of people who are bound by the same attitudes, customs and beliefs yet they distinguish them from the larger culture that it is a part of and share similar interest with. Example of this is within the larger culture of the United States, different co-cultures exist whose commonalities bond them together such as their religion, ethnicity, gender, sexual orientation, socioeconomic status, profession, or organization affiliations. How many co-culture groups can you identify with and can you find how certain values of one of your co-cultural identities conflict with the values of another?

Context

Context is where a communication event takes place. It can be viewed from the perspective of time, place, and environment being it physical or social in which the communication occurs. A broader perspective would be intrapersonal, interpersonal, small group, or mass communication. As we have covered earlier in this chapter, neither the linear nor the interaction model included the element of context, only the transaction model gives insight into what actually happens when people communicate.

Context plays an important role and can either help or harm the outcome of communication. For example, a professor having a movie as part of their lecture in a dark class with students who have had lunch before class started is probably not wise. Why? Because the students will find it more beneficial to take a nap. Arranging a meeting in a movie theater with your best friend to discuss the recent disagreement between you is not wise either. Why? Because there will be excessive noise and too many distractions for a personal conversation to take place. These two examples would serve to harm the outcome of the communication event.

When you consider context being where communication takes place, it is imperative to know it happens in these specific places; *interpersonal (communication between two people, face to face)*, *intrapersonal* (internal communication within one's self), *small groups* (communication between 3 and 20 people), and *mass communication (exchange of information on a large scale to a wide range of people through mediated channels, i.e., radio, television, and print)*.

Now that communication has been defined and each communication model including its elements has been introduced and explained, you should have a deeper understanding of the communication process and are able to implement the new skills you have learned. Let's now learn about the speech and how it all comes together.

Chapter 2

Public Speaking

Learning Objectives

Exploration in this chapter will allow students to:
2.1. Have a Better Understanding of Public Speaking
2.2. Have a Better Knowledge of Public Speakers
2.3. Know the Delivery Methods to Avoid
2.4. Define and Manage Speaker Anxiety
2.5. Understand How to Build Speaker Confidence

© Wavebreakmedia/Shutterstock.com

Dear Colleagues (A Word to Instructors)

Each new term holds its own uniqueness and each class has its own special personality, meaning that the 25 individual students enrolled in a class merge 25 different attitudes, perspectives, backgrounds, experiences, personality traits, and behaviors creating what I call a "*personality cocktail*," a mixture that yields its very own atmosphere. One class cannot be expected to be like the other even though the same subject is being taught; the "personality cocktail" sets the tone, thus dictates how the lecture is delivered, participation efforts, and chemistry between students.

© Andrey_Popov/Shutterstock.com

An instructor can teach one class with students with energy and enthusiasm and transition into the next class teaching the same subject with students demonstrating fatigue and reluctance. Therefore, it is beneficial for instructors to do an icebreaker to strengthen their students' speech legs at the very beginning of each semester on the first day of class; in the classic introduction speech, most instructors use the "bring three things that describes you method" however; the impromptu method is the one I find yields the best results.

The "three items" method in my experience was too time consuming and can't be done in one class period with 25 students (and my goal is to always optimize my class time to move on to the next assignment), then students will have to lug items to class again not to mention the students who were absent and didn't

© Andrey_Popov/Shutterstock.com

check email updates and results to using items they carry with them every day, i.e., cell phone, dorm keys, and explain the jeans they are wearing, when clearly it had nothing to do with preparing for the speech, they wore them so they would not be "naked!"

Moreover, the speech is not a major grade; it's worth only 50 point and does not merit the use of two class periods in my opinion. But I will say this . . . the one time that I used it I experienced an exquisite acoustic guitar solo from a beautiful talented student named Carlissia H . . . worth it.

The method of giving a student very short notice before taking attendance and briefing the syllabus works perfectly. You give them only two minutes to do the speech, call them in order of the alphabetical attendance system, I write what the speech should include on the board to give them a mental picture, they write it down (as it is going to be erased), and try and prepare for what they feel is the "speech of doom." The list is as follows:

- Name
- Major
- Hobbies/Interest
- What you intend to get out of the course.

Every student is taken by surprise having a speech on the first day of class and is nervous to say the least.

The students will have to gather their thoughts quickly, try to remember what the list includes; they can't write anything down to use while speaking, and the person who will go first is mortified. Trust me, there is a specific purposeful strategy to this; you see, when the student is in front of their peers of whom

© avemario/Shutterstock.com

most times they do not know, this method allows them to become familiar with each of their new classmates (getting to know their audience), which lessens the anxiety during future major speeches, now everyone knows something about the other, and a rapport has been established.

Also, it is guaranteed that many of the students will not remember the order of the list and when they began to struggle their new classmates will quietly come to their rescue and try to help them by whispering what should come next, which turns into laughter and a fun exercise. Meanwhile, there is kindness and consideration being shown among the students as well as bonds being built among them. And you professor are a rock star!

PUBLIC SPEAKING

2.1 Explaining Public Speaking

Public speaking is the art of effective oral communication with an audience. You are prone to see this done in the workplace, school, and certainly in politics. It is not at the top of most people's list of favorite things to do; however, it is a valuable skill to have and many seek to acquire training in public speaking due to the distinct advantages afforded by those who have it. Many today fear it and avoid it at all cost, however, the ancient Greeks highly valued public political participation where public speaking was an elite and cherished qualification, those that could afford it obtained education to learn how to speak with authority. The teachings of rhetoric by four ancient Greek philosophers, also known as the "fantastic four," Aspasia of Miletus (the mother of rhetoric), Socrates, Plato, and Aristotle, formulated speaker guidelines that we continue today. Roman orators Cicero and Quintilian continued the Greek rhetoric traditions as great public speakers and their contribution of written works that are still highly referenced and admired.

Helpful Insight

I want to implore you to literally see your situation for what it "really" is . . . as a classroom with students who are in the same situation as you are, an even playing field of your peers who know no more or less than you about the subject matter, there is an instructor; a situation with which you are familiar, to teach and train you on new concepts. This is neither a firing squad, nor a judge and jury; public speaking does not kill and no one is here to judge you, we are all here to learn from each other and embrace one another's ideas, culture, and perspectives; instructor included, "You" are here to "Teach Me Something" as well. I owe "you" and "you" owe me and together as a partnership we will reach success."

2.2 Understanding Public Speakers

Understanding is key in all that you do and all that you attempt to learn, so goes the process of learning public speaking; it is imperative that students understand that learning to speak in public is a learning process like any other skill set you desire, it is acquired with practice, and with practice comes confidence and with confidence comes ability. Notice that I never mentioned perfection, because one never prefects public speaking, the saying "practice makes perfect" does not apply to those who are true public speakers. The listening audience may feel that you are a master of the art when they hear your grand presentation, your powerful use of Aristotle's three artistic proofs to persuade others, ethos, logos, and pathos, as well as your command of the audience when using nonverbal concepts and so on. The truth is . . . great public speakers are never completely satisfied with their presentation and possess bundles of nerves before taking the stage; they always critique themselves afterwards as to what they wished they would have added to or taken out of their speech, they too may feel the urge to "throw up" beforehand as anyone else does. Public speakers take the stage wishing there was one minute left for completion of their speech, but from the second they are aware of or asked to a speaking engagement they are writing, researching, revising, organizing, and rehearsing as to minimize the possibility of failure because they have the same feelings of nervousness as you do. However, what they have mastered is how to use that anxiety to enhance their ability to be a great speaker as opposed to allowing the anxiety to diminish their abilities, and this is what appears to the audience as the speaker perfecting the art of public speaking. We will address those abilities further in the text, but now I will teach you about what I have developed as far as the *Delivery Methods to Avoid*, and this will also leave you with the knowledge that it is a myth that the Natural Born Public Speaker exists.

While teaching public speaking I have seen a lot of situations repeatedly that I have worked to help students to overcome or have helped them to control a particular characteristic and make it work for them as opposed to against them so I have developed these methods to avoid, so that as we study how a speech comes together we can begin by addressing pitfalls early on to maximize your potential in public speaking and minimize possibilities of failure as well.

My time in the classroom ensures that I am never void of the "wow" factor from my eager, frightened, curious, chatty, extremely reserved, as well as overzealous students. I am privileged to say that my work is never mundane neither predictable and I love that. It is during these classroom experiences that I have observed characteristics from my student speakers that have inspired these six methods to avoid. Shall we?

2.3 Delivery Methods to Avoid

1. **Sniff and Speak**
   I noticed one of my students constantly sniffy while giving their speech and it was clear that nothing needed to be sniffed up, it was so noticeable that I began to count each time he sniffed, I literally counted 28 sniffs and the speech was only two to three minutes long. When they concluded I asked the class what was the most memorable part of his speech and they said "he kept sniffing!" I now had the task of making him aware of this nervous habit of excessive sniffing, suggested that he slowed down his breathing, and when he had the urge to sniff just take a small breath instead. The student was instructed to begin his speech again while following my instructions and he executed successfully. To make one aware of a behavior they are more apt to pay closer attention to it

   © Twinsterphoto/Shutterstock.com

   and make modifications thus most times rectifying the behavior altogether. This is also useful with clearing the throat constantly while speaking. It is also considered a filler as well.

2. **Rap Hands**
   Who's your favorite rapper?... This is a trick question! Many students take nonverbal communication to a whole new level when it comes to gestures, you would think that they were performing the latest Kendrick Lamar or throwback Tupac hit, while speaking they are flailing their hands and your head is following every motion and of course the message is lost due to watching the rap hands show. Understand that gestures are important but be certain that they make sense and are appropriately timed for emphasis during speeches. Never to downplay a good rap vibe, but when speaking to an audience let's get in a Motown or classical mood and slow those hands down a bit.

   © Christian Bertrand/Shutterstock.com

3. **Militant Message**

One year when my class was scheduled to present their informative speeches, a super-smart young lady was going
to share with the class the life of a very influential woman
who had done amazing acts of kindness, and an advocate
for the underprivileged. The details of this woman's life and
work were amazing; anyone would have admired and loved
her. However, the student delivered the speech in an angry
militant way as though she was a protester rallying against
new laws or fighting for women's right to vote. Her facial ex-

© Arindambanerjee/Shutterstock.com

pression was stone, she never smiled, and her voice maintained an aggressively loud tone until the
conclusion while pounding her fist in her palm. Everyone in the class had a look of bewilderment
on their faces, they were utterly conflicted. What I read on their faces was "how am I supposed
to feel?" Am I to celebrate this woman or be frightened of her? It is the speaker that appeals to
the emotions of the audience and breathes life into the person of whom they speak, they dictate
whether the audience likes or dislikes the person or left confused. This speech was likened to a
Hulk Hogan tone delivering a lifetime achievement award speech on Betty White. The student's
delivery style separated the audience from the content itself, which also caused there to be no
balance within the verbal and nonverbal communication; they were contradicting and certainly
clashing one with the other. One has to always take into consideration the content of the message
you are trying to convey first, and thereafter you will determine your delivery method. Be certain
the method mirrors the message; do not take the picket-sign fist-pounding approach of change and
justice when sharing a message of goodwill and charity.

4. **I Know it All**

Many a new students have approached public speaking with the
"I know all" delivery method. With the thought that because
they are not shy when speaking to others, they do the announcements at church, or they are in drama class that they have nothing to learn: "I am just here to earn my three credits" is their
behavior. The ever chatty, those who always have an opinion or
comment on every subject matter, or the student that feels every
moment of silence has to be filled with their constant rambling
(as though silence will break them out in hives), are the students that will get in front of an audience and break every rule

© iQoncept/Shutterstock.com

of public speaking and feel totally offended when the assessment is not favorable. Note that having
the ability to "talk" does not make a public speaker. The greatest speakers of our time have also been
taught rules of public speaking and have honed those skills with years of practice and mistakes along
the way. One such speech was the one given by former president Bill Clinton at the 1988 Democratic
National Convention where he had delivered a famously dull
keynote address. There is trial and error, great speakers evolve
over time, and they do not become Bill Clintons overnight. So,
know-it-alls should know that they would be getting paid to
teach it if they knew it, so let me teach you and then you will
know it . . . not all!

5. **Brain Flex**

Brain Flex is one of my favorite to address with my students
because it has happened so many times. There is a method
to any professors' madness and I am no different, I stress to
my public speaking students to follow the outline sample
given precisely, i.e., the central idea, main preview, and

© Fabio Berti/Shutterstock.com

transitions etc. for a valid reason. The words written on the outline sample reflect the rubric you are being evaluated and graded from. But it never fails that a student will grab a thesaurus and substitute the words so as to sound "extra scholarly!" I stress to them that I understand that they are intelligent people but this is not the time to brain flex their broad vocabulary while I am grading them and listening for key terms nor the time to talk over the heads of their audience leaving them confused scratching their heads thinking "Oh really freshman" what the heck is *pneumonoultramicroscopicsilicovolcanoconiosis!* Remember; keep it simple, you are learning, instructions are there for your benefit. No worries though, you'll get your chance to flex that brain . . . perhaps in a creative writing class.

6. **Ceiling Audience**

   Don't be afraid of their faces! Many new student speakers begin and end their speeches with their eyes glued to the ceiling as though there is an audience up there . . . news flash, it isn't. Being in front of an audience does not give them the illusion that you are actually focused on them and where you feel it minimizes your stress level not giving eye contact, it promotes a feeling of abandonment in your audience and they also perceive you as having a lack of confidence and credibility. You have literally "filed for separation" from your audience (I'm here but we're not connecting, sort of thing)!

© edella/Shutterstock.com

   Your "real" audience is essential to the success of your presentation, your "ceiling" audience offers you nothing; no acceptance, no feedback, no benefit of learning, no appreciation, and no applause. Connect with your audience by letting them know that you are there for them and are present by looking at them through caring eyes; this adds value to your message and worth to your ever-important audience. There are people in ceilings; however, they are the magnificent painted creations of ancient European artist Michelangelo, ceiling of the Sistine Chapel in Vatican City, Rome, but not even they are applauding any speeches.

   Now that you have a leg up on *delivery methods to avoid* while preparing for the journey into public speaking, let us now explore the fundamentals of how speeches actually come together, speaker anxiety, how to build speaker confidence and how to write a memorable speech.

   Because you are students in a class, we are going to address textbook procedures but, as several of you may have postponed public speaking until your senior year, we are also going to address real-life work situations concerning speaking as well so no one gets left out and everyone's needs are met.

The Simple Truth

I feel like I'm going to throw up, I sweat under my arms, I get the bubble guts, I feel less nervous taking a hit on the football field, I literally can't breathe, I promise to have perfect attendance and do all other assignments, just please don't make me do a speech in front of the class—these statements among others have been expressed in my public speaking class from students who are literally horrified of public speaking. It is one thing that millions have in common and share the sentiment of utter fear of doing and yet it is one of the most essential things to know in society. In every aspect of one's life and/or profession, one will need to know and understand the rules of public speaking. Also, many students have the blind notion that because they are majoring in fields that are not associated with communication, they should not take the course or will not use public speaking; well, unless you are training to be The Queens Guard at Buckingham Palace you will use public speaking in every career and public speaking will make one a valuable asset to the organization in which they represent.

2.4 What Is Public Speaking Anxiety?

Many are the reactions to the fear of public speaking: feelings of nausea, cotton mouth, sweating, shaking, nervousness, and dizziness. Also, there are many terms for public speaking anxiety as well, it is defined as speech anxiety, stage fright, and communication apprehension, all of which are fear of being scrutinized or evaluated by others. No matter the name it is a frightful experience for many people. More often than not students will express that what they hope to obtain from the public speaking class is to not be nervous when speaking in the presence of others, well sorry to be the bearer of bad news but there's no guarantee of a disappearing act of nervousness any instructor can give students; however, there is the guarantee of understanding what you are dealing with emotionally and physically and the offering of techniques to help you manage your anxiety so that it will not significantly impair your ability to present a speech or presentation. Remember, in the seats around you most everyone is feeling the same way, so you are not alone.

Managing Speaker Anxiety

Extensive research has been dedicated to speaker anxiety; it is among the top things that people admit to being most afraid of, the fear is so prevalent that a study was conducted by psychologist Elizabeth Phelps and her colleagues in 2009 with 65 participants who were willing to receive a mild but unpleasant electric shock to their wrist in an effort to explore drug-free solutions that will lead to improved therapeutic treatment to unlearn and overcome phobias such as fear of giving a class presentation. It seems over the top but it speaks volumes of how serious an issue speaker anxiety really is.

Many want to know what causes this fear and how does one manage it, we already know that there is an issue with our fear of speaking but if we get an understanding of the cause we are better prepared to manage the anxiety. Now let's explore various causes of speaker anxiety.

Causes of Anxiety

1. **The Judges**
    As the definition states for speaker anxiety, we fear being scrutinized and evaluated by others, we are self-conscience in front of them, we view each one as a judge of our character and our ability. The speaker is more apt to believe the audience is there to give them a harsh sentence, when more often than not they are lenient judges only wanting you to do well and succeed, highly interested in what you have to say because they are in attendance to get something from your presentation, to them the content is far more important than you are anyway, so they are going to let you off easily, perhaps with applause at the end . . . no one is going the throw the book at anyone.

2. **Large Group Fright**
    Many admit to this being one of their main fears, they are comfortable with one-on-one communication but large groups have them shaking in their boots. Public speaking instructors hear this all the time, and never do we advise students to imagine everyone in their underwear. However, when preparing one's presentations make your speech conversational by connecting with your audience, and imagine that you have personally had one-on-one conversation with each person in attendance, that day they all just happened to be in one room. You'll then be able to present a great speech or presentation.

3. **Situation/Occasion**
    Anxiety soars for many according to the situation or occasion; being it a new or changed series of events or unexpected situations. Their nervousness goes into overdrive just knowing they will be the center of attention, the characteristics of the audience, i.e., the size, the presence of family or

colleagues, high-stakes clients, or interview of a lifetime etc. Best advice is that this anxiety does not last long and it will taper off once you have adjusted to the situation.

4. **Past Experiences**
   Anxiety toward public speaking is in many cases a learned behavior. You failed during an important presentation in the past and you have allowed the experience to alter your mindset that this tree will certainly bear the same bitter fruit as before. Nonsense! If you fall off your horse, get back on and enjoy the ride. If you know you have great content to share with an audience and you know your stuff and have put the hard work into it, there is certainly no reason for you to be crippled by a past experience. Use your intrapersonal communication skills and give yourself a positive pep talk and visualize a successful speech with great audience response and go for it. You got this!

5. **The Smell of Fear**
   You perceive that your audience knows how nervous you are and will assume you are ill prepared or unknowing of your subject matter. Your audience are people not vicious animals who are ready to attack at the smell of your fear, in fact it is just the opposite, and they are thinking "poor thing, I would be nervous up there too." Isn't that what you would think? Also remember, dress appropriately for the presentation and you will surely not look as nervous as you really are . . . professional distraction until your nerves get in check!

6. **Poorly Prepared**
   As mentioned in #4, if you have not put in hard work by doing research on your topic and audience analysis, you absolutely positively should fall flat on your face! You do an audience a disservice when you fail to prepare before coming before them, because when it comes to presentations and speeches they are what's most important in the equation. Failure due to lack of preparation on your part does nothing to promote your confidence as a public speaker and leaves only you to blame.

2.5 Building Confidence

This section will introduce you to several techniques that have been beneficial in managing natural anxiety. It is wise that you understand something very important about this section concerning building confidence; these techniques are useful but are not miracle techniques that will give you instant results but will require some work. Also, know that confidence cannot be bought, taught, or gifted to you. Confidence is built, over time step by step from our failed and successful experiences. Seek out speaking opportunities to boost your confidence level, the more you do this the more confident you will become.

Perspective

One sure way to build speaker confidence is to have things in perspective. Perspective? Yes, perspective. As you prepare for any speaking engagement, approach the situation with a full understanding of the math involved, factoring in you, the occasion, and the audience. In that equation always realize that your involvement never weighs in higher than the purpose and the audience for which you serve. Enter the task with humility and concentrate on how you are to be of service to that demographic. Also, approaching public speaking with a sincere desire to connect with your audience and not the attitude to be a "rock star" speaker with your own agenda of recognition will ensure your failures are fewer, anxiety level decreases, and confidence will be stronger.

Prepare Properly

Being prepared is quite essential in public speaking, if you seek speaker confidence. This is in fact one of the most obvious techniques, and if you dedicate the time and effort into research, organization, and diligent practice, you will increase your success and be confident that you have done what it takes to be ready. Once you have done research on your topic and put an outline together, you will then be ready to put that outline into speaking notes to practice aloud.

After you have heard your speech aloud and made your personal modifications to the speech you are ready to now practice in the presence of friends or family, insist that they give honest evaluations, and ask them to assess your tone, rate, gestures, clarity, and use of eye contact. Also, go the extra mile when preparing, make necessary copies of material for your audience, and email a copy of your presentation to yourself and the hiring agency in the event of technical issues, i.e., electronic device failures or thumb drive etc.

It is always recommended to arrive at the venue early so that you can mingle with the audience before-hand to build positive connections, which will prove beneficial for using great eye contact when speaking.

Preparation also means, being body wise. If you plan and prepare sufficiently leading up to the presen-tation, procrastination is not an issue nor last minute late night cramming the night before, as that should be reserved for a good night's sleep, a brisk walk in the morning as well as a balanced breakfast. This will also, lessen speaker anxiety and build one's confidence.

Presence and Authenticity

When one is presenting, these are the most important when it comes to oral communication techniques. A speaker must rely on every means of expression, your job is never to just deliver information but to create experience and influence based on the message by drawing from one's physical presence, voice, gestures, as well as content. Your presence should tell the audience that you are the expert authority, it should command their attention, as well as make them feel they are in capable trusting hands.

Skills Training

In whatever you desire to do professionally, invest in skills training to ensure your rate of success. Concerning public speaking and speaker anxiety can you imagine a better confidence builder than being professionally trained in speech writing, organization, and delivery techniques? A study by Duff and colleagues (2007) states that enrolling in a communication course that teaches public speaking skills was as successful in reducing speaker anxiety as other treatment methods. Studying and applying the points given in this text should serve as a great tool to building your speaker confidence.

Know the Venue

Arrive early before your audience I suggest and become familiar with the room in which you will be speak-ing. Get a feel for where the audience will be sitting, stand behind the lectern, get a quick tutorial on how to operate the technology for visual presentations, and check the microphones for sound and height specifica-tions. Also, walk from where you will be sitting to where you will be speaking to assess ease of access and minimal distractions while maneuvering.

Relaxation and Diaphragmatic Breathing

For a successful speech outcome you must first relax. Relaxation is the state of being free of tension and anxiety. There are many types of relaxation techniques to reduce anxiety and promote other health benefits such as one called *autogenic relaxation*, according to the Mayo Clinic it is a form of relaxation which means something that comes from within you. In this relaxation technique, you use both visual imagery and body awareness to reduce stress.

© lenetstan/Shutterstock.com

You repeat words or suggestions in your mind to relax and reduce muscle tension. For example, you may imagine a peaceful setting and then focus on controlled, relaxing breathing, slowing your heart rate, or feeling different physical sensations, such as relaxing each arm or leg one by one. Once you have reached that level of relaxation you should then imagine yourself successfully delivering your speech, getting a positive response from your audience followed by an excited applause of a speech well done at the end.

What a natural function is breathing, we do it without thinking about it; however, we must lend greater attention to it in public speaking just as professional singers, spoken word artist, and voice actors. Proper breathing methods is a function one has to retrain themselves to do if they want to be successful at public speaking as well; one such method is *diaphragmatic breathing*, which is defined as abdominal breathing, belly breathing, or deep breathing, which is breathing that is done by contracting the diaphragm, a muscle located horizontally between the thoracic cavity and abdominal cavity. Air enters the lungs and the belly expands during this type of breathing, now you are to practice breathing slower, deeper, and calmer while controlling your exhalation so you are able to support the sound to the end of phrases where the most powerful words are and your voice projection can be heard by those in the back of the room.

Positive Visualization

One could not fathom Serena Williams preparing for a tennis match by visualizing low percentage of serves, not getting the high points, or her opponent winning Wimbledon; negative visualization would not have made her the Wimbledon champion on July 9, 2016 achieving a historic 22nd Grand Slam title. There is no question that to be able to amass that level of success Williams has to keep her confidence strong by using positive visualization; seeing herself beforehand on the grass executing powerfully and winning the prize. It would be ridiculous to imagine it happening any other way wouldn't it? Yet most public speakers will imagine themselves extremely nervous, sweating, or drawing a blank. If this sounds familiar, then you should definitely retrain your brain to start using positive visualization, use images that are positive and work for you and not against you, see yourself at the event poised, polished, and prepared. See yourself mingling with other attendees who are expressing enthusiasm about hearing you speak, see great audience responses, an effective delivery and everyone applauding as you conclude.

© Patrick Tuohy/Shutterstock.com

Positive images such as these will boost your confidence and on the actual day you give your presentation it will be as though you have already done this before because you have recorded these positive images and now you expect to have the successful outcome you visualized.

Do It Again

Do you want your fear to totally go away?... Forget about it! But what can certainly boost your confidence and sharpen your speaking skills is to "do it again," the more experience the less anxiety you will feel. This course is designed with structured assignments to enhance your speaking skill set by writing and actually presenting speeches which will build your confidence and help you acquire frequent practice. Research shows that students who practice often report an increase in general confidence as well as a marked sense of achievement. Many students get incredibly nervous the first time they have to do a speech in front of their classmates but with practice the nerves subside and they usually begin to enjoy the whole process. Moreover, in addition to the practice in the classroom it is highly recommended to seek out speaking opportunities from organizations you are affiliated with on campus, or join organizations dedicated to public speaking that will help you hone your skills in an environment of supportive professionals.

Being Audience Centered

Building your confidence involves having the wherewithal to know you must be audience centered. If you are being *audience centered* it implies that you are focused on the audience to be able to know if they understand your concepts and ideas rather than focusing merely on how everything directly affects you. Many times if you are more focused on the performance of the speech you will become more nervous than you actually need to be. This is not about you or your "moment to shine," this is about being centered indeed; however, audience–centered, not self-centered. Remember, your main concern should be the needs of your audience, how the speech will help and be beneficial to the lives of others. Something valuable all speakers should know is that the reason people attend such events is that they have a need in the first place and are looking for answers of hope, inspiration, and change thus they have arrived with a level of anxiety of their own so if you keep their needs ahead of your own you'll soon wonder when yours disappeared.

What I Know Now

- What Public Speaking Is
- Insight on Public Speakers
- Delivery Methods to Avoid
- I Know about Public Speaking Anxiety
- I Know about Building Speaker Confidence

Chapter 3

The Speech and How It All Comes Together

Learning Objectives

Exploration in this chapter will allow students to:
3.1. Understand the Various Delivery Methods
3.2. Determine Your Purpose
3.3. Demonstrate the Steps to Preparing a Speech
3.4. Understand the Importance of Being Audience Centered
3.5. Organize a Speech in Outline Form

© KarSol/Shutterstock.com

God, that all-powerful Creator of nature and architect of the world, has impressed man with no character so proper to distinguish him from other animals, as by the faculty of speech.

— Quintilian

Jay works for a major company within the oil and gas industry as a financial analyst. His department is compiled of several teams servicing various overseas accounts, and each team works in collaboration with the other according to the needs of the client. He has been a member of the same team for four years and is known to be a team player and very good at his job. Recently his department went through some restructuring and he was reassigned to another team; this change was unwelcomed as Jay has experienced some unpleasant encounters with the supervisor of this new team.

Scenario

© Andrey_Popov/Shutterstock.com

He has observed the supervisor being rude, unprofessional, and insulting to colleagues, so much so that some team members reported the supervisor to HR and requested to be placed on other teams. Jay is going into this team not favoring this new supervisor at all.

Being an analyst he is no stranger to giving presentations to groups even though he is usually a quiet and reserved person; however, it is a part of his job and he excels in it. Knowing Jay's skill set at giving presentations his colleague Daniel came by his office to share details of a humanitarian's awards ceremony to be held next week for the new supervisor. Jay listens intently and professionally states "that's quite an honor she must be pleased." Absolutely, replies Daniel, "we have all chose various roles to plan an exciting event and we have saved the honor of preparing and delivering the speech for you!" Jay is shocked but tries really hard not to show any signs of disapproval to avoid raising any suspicion in Daniel.

It is clear that Jay has a dilemma, while understanding the rules of public speaking we will discuss some of the issues he faces further in this chapter.

3.1 Delivery Methods See Figure 3.1

It is the vast hope of many speakers that once they began their speech the dreaded anxiety they feel will dissipate. One thing is for certain, that if you persist your confidence will surface and usher you gracefully to the end. However, the way it is received by your listeners will rely heavily on the delivery method one chooses to use. Below we will address in detail the four ways you can deliver a speech: memorization, manuscript, impromptu, and extemporaneous.

Figure 3.1 Delivery Methods

Extemporaneous

Manuscript

Delivery Methods

Memorized

Impromptu

Memorization

Memorized method is when you write out a speech beforehand and repeatedly rehearse it until you commit the entire text to memory. Attempting to deliver a word for word speech is usually the most appealing to the novice speaker and is certainly the most difficult.

However, impressive experts advise against this method as there are several disadvantages to it. The memorized method puts too much pressure on the speaker; if the novice speaker's main focus is keeping his words from falling out of his head, he will more than likely appear mechanical and his anxiety will not dissipate during his speech as it would with other methods.

Another huge disadvantage of this method is that it is hard to do well. Perfect execution at home in a mirror or in the presence of a family member does not mean your memory will not fail you in the presence of a live audience filled with people of whom you are not familiar (a common disappointment for inexperienced speakers). Usually when this happens the speakers' only recourse to get back on track is to start their speech over from the beginning . . . an unmistakable sign to the audience that they are listening to an amateur speaker who attempted to memorize their speech.

Speakers will also miss important aspects of speech delivery using this method such as the ability to interact with the audience members, assess their understanding of the content, or interpret or respond to their feedback. Tuning into and reading the audience for expressions of disagreement or frowns of confusion could be overlooked by speaker for the sake of getting through his presentation without distraction.

Memorized delivery is however, appropriate for professional speakers like evangelist and politicians because they use the same speech frequently only modifying it when the audience changes.

Manuscript

This method is when a speaker reads his speech from a prepared text; you write the speech out beforehand and then you read the speech aloud to an audience. For the novice speaker it is a preferred choice because of the security it provides; to give accurate details throughout the speech for easy reference. This has similar drawbacks as the memorized method. When you are reading a speech you are communicating with the paper and not the audience, therefore there is no interaction with them, the speech cannot be conversational or natural and will lack interest, becoming monotonous. While reading a speech the speaker is on a set course and opportunities for speech enhancement by deviation or spontaneous audience engagement as well as the use of important expressiveness and body language does not exist. These are all actually the components that make speeches successful in the first place.

One has to be an exceptional writer (which is not the case for many) to pull this method off, otherwise it is usually a grave mistake to read verbatim.

Exceptions to this rule are reserved for presidents of the United States, who have some of the greatest writers on staff. Inexperienced writers run the risk of sounding dull and stiff when reading what they have written.

Impromptu Delivery

This is when you speak off-the-cuff, the speech is done without being planned, organized, or rehearsed. Indulging in everyday interactions with others is impromptu speaking; however, in other situations it is a ground for panic. For example, students dread being called upon in class, a parishioner may get nauseated when called to welcome new guests to Sunday service, or an employee put on the spot at a staff meeting to explain a new policy could become inarticulate.

The normalcy of everyday conversations may provide plenty of practice in impromptu speaking but is certainly not enough to avoid the feelings of acute self-consciousness many experience when suddenly called on to speak before an audience.

Being a speaker at some point you may be asked to do this type of speaking, and if so its elements will consist of a condensed version of any prepared speech of general communication. And if you are an experience speaker you may do quite well at impromptu speaking, being able to come across sincere and knowledgeable on varied topics, although to do so it is recommended that you have a few brief speeches in your arsenal for such speaking.

It is highly impressive when someone is able to "think on their feet" and speak confidently when called on the spur of the moment then executing with organized thoughts and ideas it speaks volumes of one's skills and credibility.

Extemporaneous

Don't memorize! Don't recite! Don't by any means call me without warning! Well what else do we have . . . extemporaneous speaking, the most common and highly recommended method of speech delivery, the one that works best for most speakers.

It requires one to be well prepared yet every single word is not etched in stone. It is designed for practicing with notes from the very beginning from the written and researched outline of your topic. Frequent practice is never for memorization but to become familiar with content with expression and seamless flow of ideas. Don't memorize; familiarize! Notes are only to highlight key points and important facts that are difficult to remember such as date, figures, sources etc.

Although you are speaking extemporaneously, you will still incorporate techniques from the other methods as well. Some portions of your speech should be memorized like the opening, transitions, and the conclusion; this ensures that you know how to get from point to point and are maintaining eye contact at every important moment of your speech. There will be moments when you will read from your notes to navigate you through the process as well as tossing some impromptu remark in for good measure.

Rest assured that this method affords you with the possibility to present a dynamic speech as you will be able to use gestures, maintain appropriate eye contact with your audience, and move on stage, which promotes in captivating listeners' attention.

You can count on the luxury of flexibility with this delivery method as well, which keeps you in control and relaxed in knowing you know where you are going and the means in which you are going to arrive.

3.2 General Purpose

You are now informed on the common delivery methods for presenting a speech but equally as important is understanding the purpose or goal for which you are speaking to an audience, *the general purpose*. Speeches are prepared for one of three general purposes, you must consider what effect you want to have on your audience members, is to *inform*, *persuade*, or to *entertain*. If it is your intent to inform an audience you may want to inform them on issues or bring awareness and understanding. When you select a subject matter to speak on, you are taking on a role to teach and impart valuable knowledge. This could be about a concept, person, event, thing, place, or problem. The informative speech could be to expand existing knowledge of a topic with new research or developments to an audience or an entirely new concept. To inform, a speaker must be certain to provide listeners with sound, concise, and accurate detailed facts about the topic. Also, if a speaker is to be successful in their efforts to inform, they must show the audience signs that they possess credibility; they must be willing and able to believe what you are presenting to them; buy what you are selling so to speak.

Do you hope to persuade an audience to change their belief about something? If so, understand that this is in no way easy for a speaker to achieve and certainly not during one speech. After all, the reason for *persuasive speech* is to influence the values, beliefs, attitudes, or behaviors of others; certainly people generally frown upon attempts to influence their beliefs or change their behaviors and/or ideas about things. However, many topics of controversy require speakers to do just that, and you are to take a position on an issue and advocate a policy, cause, idea, or product. The speaker may attempt to convince the public against Senate Bill 11, campus carry, want to sell the next iPhone, or that all new police officers receive advanced training, background checks, and are strategically assigned to neighborhoods. Whatever the topic, the speakers' purpose is to get an audience to think, see, and feel differently; take action; do more as a result of their speech, not to just agree.

So you want to entertain them? Being that your speeches will be more to inform or persuade this text is geared more toward those two methods; however, to prepare a *speech to entertain* is no small feat, and is prepared most times to keep an audience in a jovial and lighthearted mood. It is usually for after-dinner entertainment and is not required very often, and can be one of great difficulty as well. When the speakers' job is to make the audience laugh, they are indeed faced with a great challenge; because humor is not universal, their responsibility is to consider humor that is culturally appropriate, tasteful for the occasion and audience. Remember it is always a safe bet to talk about issues that everyone can relate to, like funny family situations, i.e., weird teenage behavior, birth of a child, in-laws, your crazy uncle Puncho, annoying little sisters or work, pets, travel, or your arch nemesis "the next door neighbor from hell!"

Moreover, steer clear of topics that will easily offend audience members such as; politics, religion, race, sports teams, and sexual orientation. Also, skilled speakers will have their talk prepared beforehand and would never resort to getting through it at the expense of the audience; meaning using them as the brunt of jokes or punch lines, you will not be a favored guest and will be cited for unprofessionalism, no tact, and certainly no returns.

Now that it is clear what the general purpose is, we are ready to learn the steps to preparing a speech from beginning to end.

3.3 Steps to Preparing a Speech

Steps to preparing a speech and knowing which step is most important.

Getting a speech together is a skill set in and of itself. There are specific variables that must be in place in order for this to be done successfully; first you must conduct an audience analysis, select a topic, research, organize an outline, rehearse, and deliver.

Next we will look into each step in an effort to prepare you in the likely event your instructor elects to give you the responsibility of presenting a speech during this course. Hopefully you will find the steps helpful and the tools something that will prove instrumental far beyond this public speaking class.

Step 1. Audience Analysis See Figure 3.2

The first and most important step is your *audience analysis*, because this step is central to all other decisions related to preparing a speech and greatly influences every aspect of the other five steps. In the preparation of a speech, *audience analysis* is the process of determining the values, interests, and attitudes

Figure 3.2 Six Steps to a Powerful Speech

Step 1. Audience Analysis

Step 2. Select a Topic

Step 3. Research

Step 4. Organize an Outline

Step 5. Rehearse

Step 6. Deliver your Speech

of the intended or projected listeners. Certainly in this course your audience is a captive one, you are already knowledgeable of who they are (students) and why they are here (to successfully pass the course). That of course gives you an advantage but in real corporate situations where you may be hired as keynote speaker there are specifics you must know about your audience and they are as follows:

© Monkey Business Images/Shutterstock.com

- The genders of your audience, the percentage of male and female represented in audience
- The age range of your audience members
- Marital status
- Are they parents
- Educational background
- Socioeconomic statues
- Geographic location of audience
- Varied ethnic backgrounds represented in audience
- Living situation; in own apartment, at home with parents, in a dorm, homeowners

This systematic way of gathering information about your audience will allow you to know who they are, what their interest are, and why they are here. These are general demographics needed for you to plan your topic and research to cater to that specific group of people, having done this most intricate step first will ensure the next five steps go smoothly. When speakers fail to do this first step they can expect negative outcomes in their desired speaker goals being met.

Step 2. Selecting Your Topic

The second step is to select a topic, which appears to be a challenge for many students. In your course your general purpose will be assigned to you by your instructor, i.e., informative or your persuasive speech, but most times you will have to choose a topic that reflects that general purpose. This simple advice is key in selecting a topic; start with "you" first, your life experiences, hobbies, interest, travels, and if they are of interest to you they will be of interest to others. Some text will tell you not to discard any topic that topics for the most part are not boring it is "Speakers not topics make for fascinating presentations." Well, some would beg to differ, many students will quickly go to their cell phones and pull up informative or persuasive speech topics . . . do understand that your professors have heard so many speeches over the course of their careers that they practically know all those speeches when students present them for topic ideas and many professors absolutely refuse to continue listening to them.

Not saying that many of them are not important but they are definitely over-done and considered "tired topics." Examples; Drinking and Driving, Texting and Driving, Organ Donation, Domestic Violence, Gun Control, Blood Donation, Legalizing Marijuana and the list goes on and on, some text will provide "Suggested Speech Topics" but because you are commissioned to start with "you" when selecting a topic there is no way of knowing what vast interesting and exciting topics will unfold so we will provide you with a "Tired Topic" list to avoid instead, accompanied by definition, explanations, and justifications if one such topic must be used.

Tired Topics

What is a Tired Topic? They lead to Thesis Statements that have been done lots of times by lots of students. Therefore, it is extremely difficult to give a new, original, creative speech on such a topic. They can be discussed for several minutes without doing much (or any) research. They are topics for which it is difficult to give any new information or arguments. *Most Tired Topic speeches don't show off your research and reasoning skills sufficiently to earn a grade of A or B.* Lots of "Free Term Paper" or "Great Speech Topic" websites provide mediocre samples on these topics (which, unfortunately, many students plagiarize and earn an automatic zero). If I ask you why you chose a topic and your answer is some variation of "This is all I could think of," odds are it's a Tired Topic.

Any Proposal, Outline, or Speech even vaguely related to these topics MUST be accompanied by an *additional 300-word typed justification essay* explaining how this speech will be different from all the other speeches on this topic. What "new news," new perspectives, etc., does your speech offer on a topic that has been covered multiple times by multiple people? This essay MUST demonstrate a significant specific difference between your treatment of this topic and previous speeches on this topic. You will be assessed a grade penalty on any proposals, outlines, or speeches given on listed Tired Topics unaccompanied by the justification essay. The justification essay does not count as extra credit or earn any points.

Examples are given below in order to give you some idea of what topics to avoid. This is not an exhaustive list. Just because a topic is not listed here does NOT automatically mean it is acceptable. If there is even the slightest similarity between your topic and one on this list, check with your instructor, propose a different topic, or else include a 300-word typed justification essay with your topic proposal, outline, or speech.

Abortion	Etiquette	Stock Market
Affirmative Action/ Proposition 209	Euthanasia	Sickle Cell Anemia
	Exercise types (Yoga, etc.)	Suicide
AIDS	Exercise/Stay fit	Sun Tanning
Anorexia/Bulimia	Fraternities and Sororities	Surrogate Parents
Athletes (biography, "best player," etc.)	Giving Blood	Tattoos
	Gun Control	Technology/the Internet
Attention Deficit Disorder	Hair care, styles, etc.	Television (sex and/or violence)
Body image, weight, and beauty standards	Legalizing Drugs	
	Marijuana (Uses, Legalization, etc.)	Texting while driving
Bullying, Cyber-bullying		Time Management/ Procrastination
CPR	Motorcycle/Bicycle Safety	
Cancer	Natural hair, Relaxed hair	Title IX
Capital Punishment	Nutrition	Sex Ed./Birth Control
Cloning	Organ Donation	Teenage Pregnancy
Coke vs Pepsi/Taste Tests	Personal Grooming	Stress
Conspiracy Theories	Rape	Video games (and violence)
Diabetes	Recycle	Volunteer for community service
Dieting	Religious Topics	
Diseases and Disorders	Musicians/Groups/Bands	Voting
Drinking Age	Seatbelts	Drugs (risks, legalizing, other uses, etc.)
Drinking and Driving	Smoking/Chewing Tobacco	
Drink more water	Speed Limits	
Energy or Gatorade drinks	Sports (how to, rules, etc.)	

ANY "Disease or Disorder" topic

Speeches on disease-related topics invariably follow the "cause, effect, cure/prevent" pattern, and thus all start to sound alike. Claiming that your speech will focus more on a new cure or treatment is not sufficient. That angle has been used multiple times by multiple students. Such speeches usually devolve into the "cause, effect, cure/prevent" format by the time they reach the outline stage.

ANY persuasive speech topic with which the audience already agrees. For example, persuading the audience that it would be a good thing to:

Volunteer for community service
Recycle
Exercise/Stay fit/Diet
Vote
Etc.

ANY Special Occasion or Ceremonial Speech discussing how a person "overcame obstacles" through "hard work" and "determination." They all start to sound alike. Only the names change.

The idea is to promote creativity, originality, and a sincere effort in the topic selection, many universities have implemented systems for students to upload a body of their work into the universities' archives in the event that a student will go on to graduate school, the speech will be available for the student to use for extended research on their thesis. For reasons like this you would want to avoid uploading a "tired topic" with little or no originality. Food for thought.

Step 3. Research

Step 3 is research, the process of gathering your supporting material, which will make the difference in whether the audience will believe and accept the perspective you bring to the topic.

Research is designed to help you define, clarify, illustrate, and support your position. As stated in Step 2, start with "you" and what you already know about the topic and then use research to add new elements to a topic with which you are already familiar. Your main goal at this point is to find material that will add interest to your topic and bring insight into areas that may need clarity to your audience. Remember you are your first source, then you search various databases found in the library for scholarly articles, you may consult the experts, conduct interviews, and you can also find articles in reputable magazines and newspapers.

Step 4. Organizing Your Outline

The research is done, which aids in ensuring familiarity of content, now we have to organize it and put it in outline format, this part seems a bit complex; however, it is a necessary evil and time and effort must be given to it to be able to successfully deliver your speech.

When preparing to organize the research you have gathered for your topic you then must put your topic into a particular structure, all speeches have three parts: a beginning, a middle, and an end. We will refer to these as the *introduction,* the *body,* and the *conclusion* and we will undertake a closer examination of these further in the text. However, for the time being this will prove enough to demonstrate that each speech includes certain components that serve particular functions. (Outline samples will be addressed further in the text.)

The Introduction

Each Introduction should be designed to (1) get the audience's attention, (2) state listener relevance, (3) speaker credibility, (4) central idea, and (5) initial preview of main points, which in most cases should be three main points, any more than that could confuse your audience.

To get your audience's attention consider these attention getting devices in order to do so:

1. The appropriateness and relevance to the audience (consider cultures and backgrounds)
2. Purpose of speech (Inform, persuade, or entertain)

3. Topic (have relevant connection to your speech)
4. Occasion (occasions will determine different tones, or particular styles or manners of speaking)

Listener Relevance

This is when you share a statement of how and why your speech relates to or might affect your audience.

Speaker Credibility

There are several important stages of credibility students need to be aware of as they began the study of public speaking, first to define what credibility is.

Credibility is, literally, the extent to which your audience believes you when you speak. It is about the trust they place in you, especially as being an expert in your topic. Unlike simple trust, which is often given until a person is found untrustworthy, credibility often has to be earned, and people will look first to indicators such as achievements in education and employment, then to their first-hand experience of your presentation.

Initial Credibility

Initial credibility is that which you have before the presentation. This may be zero when people do not know you at all. It may also be very high if you are a known author, professor, or personality who has achieved fame.

For those with low initial credibility, the task is to create credibility, which is where presented credibility is important and particularly derived credibility for real evidence.

For those with high initial credibility, the challenge is to live up to expectations, which may be artificially inflated, perhaps by your publicists or maybe by excessive admiration from your adoring audience!

Presented Credibility

That which is presented to the audience before you speak. If there is a brief biography in event material, then this may give them some indication of your achievements.

A powerful form of presented credibility is a glowing reference from other people who themselves have high credibility. This is often done when a known person introduces a person who is not known.

Things that add to presented credibility include:
- High qualifications, such as a PhD or degrees in multiple subjects.
- Having books and papers published.
- Senior positions in known organizations.
- Significant achievements in your work or private life.

Derived Credibility

Comes from what you actually present. It comes from the quality of the material in your presentation, including the layout of your slides and the credibility of the facts you present. It comes from the words you use and how you say them. It also comes from how you dress and present yourself with clear authority.

A person with high initial credibility can lose significant credibility here if they are ill-prepared, which can happen to a famous person with an over-busy schedule. If your audience thinks you do not care enough about them, then they may feel betrayed and discount much of what you say.

A person with low initial credibility can do a lot here to build credibility with a clear, well-thought-out presentation and strong delivery. It does not have to be world-class as your audience likely does not expect this. But if you send them away with a good impression of both you and what you have said, your credibility will take a significant boost.

Terminal Credibility

Is that which your audience takes away with them. Perhaps unfairly, if they admire you already, they may forgive you for a less than perfect display (although this is a dangerous game to play).

Equally unfair, they may forget what a lesser-known speaker says, even though it is sound. This is one reason why it is important to make a solid and clear impact, not over-doing it nor presenting too much information. They will remember few things, so do remember to make your points clear and to give them a strong ending (Straker 2010).

Central Idea

This is one concise sentence that summarizes the speech content, the central idea sentence is the "bite size" version of your speech—your entire speech in just one sentence.

Central Idea Examples:
- Homelessness in America is increasing daily and the impact is weighing heavier on our veterans.
- Volunteer English teaching programs exist in almost all corners of the world; however, the demands for volunteer teachers are high but the supply is quite low.
- Yo-Yo dieting has taken the place of proper nutrition and exercise for many Americans, which for them is costly and promotes risk to their overall health.
- Teaching at a US Department of Defense school is much like teaching at a school within the United States and teachers should explore the opportunity.

These examples should serve as useful tools to help you create your central ideas with ease and understanding; once you have your central idea, use it to develop your main points.

Preview of Main Points

Having the right topic, purpose, and properly worded central idea, the next important task is to develop your main points. As stated earlier, you should have no more than three main points, otherwise it could confuse your audience or perhaps just be too long and drawn out (which will lose the audience interest). Developing solid main points depends greatly on that well-written central idea, and from it you should come up with main points that speaks of why the central idea is true, it should let your audience know what to expect in your speech, as well as if it can be supported with points that bring interest and value to an audience. Moreover, the main points should add life to and transition naturally into the body of the speech.

Example of Central Idea and Main Points Together
(**Central Idea**) Teaching at a US Department of Defense school is much like teaching at a school within the United States and teachers should explore the opportunity.

(**Main Points**) Therefore, it is (1) important to know the application process, (2) teaching categories and requirements, (3) and the benefits of teaching abroad.

*Note; A complete thesis statement, includes central idea and initial preview of main points, three main points for proper building of the body of the outline. Below is how it should appear in the outline.

Teaching at a US Department of Defense school is much like teaching at a school within the United States and teachers should explore the opportunity. Therefore, it is important to know the application process, teaching categories and requirements, and the benefits and teaching abroad.

Now that you know the steps to organizing your outline, it is time to rehearse for your speech.

Step 5. Rehearse

There are several ways people use to practice their speeches.

It is time to rehearse for a successful delivery of your speech. Being that you will be speaking extemporaneously, your practicing will ensure you become more familiar with the concepts and ideas by talking them through. You will be doing your initial practice from your preparation outline, therefore you are reading the concepts verbatim as they are written. After several times with this approach you will be more secure with the content and will not need to say the exact same thing each time as now you know the material well enough that the thoughts will come to you easier and will flow more naturally.

Many speakers start rehearsing in front of a mirror with their preparation outline, which is great as this allows you to observe yourself using appropriate gestures, eye contact, good posture and vocals. Pay attention to see if you are mindful to smile during practice, this is important because it relaxes you and your audience, giving off feelings of warmth and acceptance, which also eases the speaker's anxiety.

© Glaze Image/Shutterstock.com

You have mastered the mirror and the use of the preparation outline now it is time to record yourself and listen to your delivery, (this comes easy because there is a recording function on everyone's mobile device so there is no inconvenience following this practice step).

Once recorded, listen to see if you are speaking with clarity, with appropriate rate and tone, if you are using emphasis when needed especially when addressing your main points, if you hear that you are not delivering strongly during your thesis statement then modifications are to be made at once to present it more dynamically. Try tweaking your vocal delivery, make transitions stronger, or you may have to rearrange the main points.

You started out practicing with your preparation outline now that you are more familiar with the content and made modifications to your recorded practice, you are now ready to begin practicing with your presentation outline . . . this is the one that is boiled down to fit on an index card. Where only key information and words are printed to trigger the familiar content and derives the same statements made while practicing when you followed the preparation outline. Incorporate the efforts of friends at this point to listen to your speech several times and give honest critiques, make those adjustments and voila you are ready to deliver your speech.

Useful Information

Many students will micro-print their entire speech on their index cards and turn a supposedly extemporaneous speech into a manuscript speech by reading the audience a story. This is problematic because it is easy to lose their place, which provokes long pauses while searching; further, they are not able to use nonverbal communication and this usually bores the audience, thus the speaker loses credibility not to mention the heightened anxiety this causes the speaker as well.

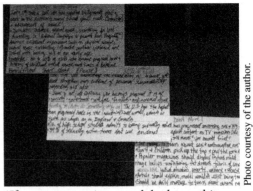

*If your presentation speech looks anything like this, you are setting yourself up for failure.

Photo courtesy of the author.

Step 6. Delivery

There is indeed an art to a masterful introduction to a speech . . . what might that be you ask . . . commit it to memory! Yes that is true, extemporaneous speaking allows the incorporation of several methods during your speech and the introduction and the conclusion should be developed in exact wording and executed with precision.

It is a certain agitation to observe a speaker mulling over notes during an introduction as if to be seeing the information for the first time, it is imperative that for these 30–45 seconds you connect with your audience, draw them in by looking in their faces exacting the knowledge of what has been prepared for them, letting them know that you have arrived with their needs in mind and are now one with them. Significant importance lies in your introduction and conclusion, the two determine the first and last impression the audience has of the speaker.

Having a sense of how you will start will give you confidence and knowing your conclusion will ensure you do not have to scramble for memorable closings. It is the body of the speech that should undoubtedly be presented extemporaneously, which will make it more effective as you will then use the presentation outline to draw on those key words.

3.4 The Importance of Being Audience Centered

You have arrived anticipating hearing from me. Make no mistake . . . I know who's starring in this scene . . . It has always been you . . . the Audience.

— *Authors own*

The successful speech is the one written with the audience in mind from start to finish. When the writer can take himself out of the equation, considering only the needs, hopes, and values of the audience, he is one who has the recipe for effective delivery. This is due to the commitment to professional skills training, a passion for service and the advancement of others.

A speaker who has done the homework of properly conducting an audience analysis, that audience will actually write the speech that is to be written.

The speaker should always present themselves ethically and be mindful of the audience interest, and their situation. Audience members' cultures and diversities should be respected; the speaker should always be all inclusive never isolating anyone, and never singling out any particular demographic.

A skillful speaker should be able to construct a speech that speaks of hope, inspiration, and love and never mention any particular religion, speak of brotherhood, charity, and goodwill and never indicate race, nationality, or country. Speakers are the adhesive that binds a people together and provokes them to become servers one to another. Trustworthiness is what is freely offered to the audience in which they serve.

No matter what the make-up of the audience is or the situation in which the speaker has to speak their professional obligation should rise to the occasion.

Figure 3.3 Sample Outline Format

Format for Speech Outline
Topic:
Specific Purpose:
INTRODUCTION
A. Attention Getter
B. Relevance
C. Credibility
D. Thesis Statement
Transition:
I.   Body
A. Main point 1 Recap Statement
1. Supporting Material (5 complete sentences including a source)
2. Supporting Material
Transition
II. Main point 2 Recap Statement
1. Supporting Material (5 complete sentences including a source)
2. Supporting Material
Transition
III. Main point 3 Recap Statement
1. Supporting Material (5 complete sentences including a source)
2. Supporting Material
CONCLUSION
Transition to Closing:
A. Final Summary
B. Memorable Closing
References

Let's refer back to our scenario at the beginning of this chapter when Jay was asked by his colleagues to present a speech for the supervisor that he thought less than professional. If speakers are to always be audience centered and put the needs of them first how do you think he should handle this situation?

Should he:
1. Decline to do it.
2. Share his opinion about the supervisor to his colleagues.
3. Prepare a short speech with documented facts of accomplishments.
4. Turn on the charm and deceive the audience as though he and the supervisor were besties.

*Instructors indulge your class in a discussion on the possible outcomes of the scenario.

3.5 Organize a Speech in Outline Form

We have covered many steps in this chapter to address how the speech comes together; however, this chapter would not be complete without an outline sample to assist the student in preparation for the speech writing process. Below is a sample format for a speech outline.

Chapter 4

Narrowing Your Topic and Acquiring Supporting Material

Learning Objectives

Exploration in this chapter will allow students to discover:

4.1. What Guidelines Should Be Followed When Selecting a Topic?
4.2. How to Narrow Your Topic.
4.3. What Resources Are Available When Researching Topics?
4.4. What Types of Supporting Materials Are Used in Speeches?

© Dean Drobot/Shutterstock.com

Seek to do a thing right the first time to counter the mistakes of a lifetime.

—Authors own

Missy listened attentively in class during her professor's lecture on selecting a topic; she took notes about beginning with one's hobbies or things of interest to you but found it difficult to relate to those guidelines and became quite nervous. It was a summer course and she knew that the course moved quickly and the content had to be absorbed, retained, and then demonstrated just as quickly, which made her anxiety about the speech grow even more.

Scenario

© Monkey Business Images/Shutterstock.com

She really wanted to do well but was not sure if she could follow through on selecting a suitable topic that her fellow students would find interesting. Class was dismissed, however, her feelings of uncertainty were not; they accompanied her throughout the remainder of the day, she thought of topic after topic and nothing seemed to make since.

Missy knew she had but one solution . . . expose her feelings of defeat to her professor and ask for help. The next morning she arrived a bit earlier and approached her professor: "Good morning Dr. LaBelle, may I speak to you concerning my topic?" she said, wringing her hands. "Hello Missy, you certainly may, what can I do for you?" replied professor LaBelle. "Well I just can't come up with a topic, it's nearly impossible!" she exclaimed, rolling her eyes. "Impossible?" her professor asked, with a puzzled look on her face. "Yes impossible, because you said we should start with our hobbies and things of interest to us but the problem is you see I only go the school, work, home, and I have no hobbies so that would constitute my not being very interesting either," she cried. Looking over her glasses, professor LaBelle said firmly, "I hear what you're saying but my processor say's 'Non-sense!' She continued, "Do you have a pulse? Are your breathing? You have a family? Are you dating? Have any friends? Did any traveling?"

Missy looked amused at her professor and said "yes" to all of the questions except the one about "Are you dating?" Then she excitedly replied, "Oh my family and I went to Haiti for vacation!" Missy and professor LaBelle both erupted into laughter as she had her light bulb moment and revelation of her being extremely interested in a topic that she knew would be perfect for her audience.

****

Speech day is a day that the classroom is filled with students' wearing the fragrance of anxiety and perspiration, however, not inspired by Chanel. The sounds of dreaded huffs, last minute preparations of stapling papers, revising note cards and finishing touches on their visual aids bounce off the walls as their professor observes while monitoring the clock on the back wall . . . two minutes until Showtime.

This atmosphere is in fact the norm in any public speaking class on speech day, as well as pleas to the instructor to change the order in which the speakers will be called. Moreover, before this day something important has to take place . . . the topic has to be selected. We covered much of this in Chapter 3 as part of the steps in preparing a speech, therefore we will now expound on some guidelines and narrowing one's topic in this chapter.

4.1 Guidelines to Selecting a Topic

Consider the Audience

Never by any means fail to neither consider your audience, nor underestimate them, to do such will be to any speaker's detriment. Many veteran speakers' calendars are full, their names are highly recognized, they have a team handling their appearance schedule, and business is good. In the lieu of all this they often lose sight of what should always be their main objective "the audience" as they begin to feel that they have mastered the "act" not "art" of public speaking and commence to delivering stale duplicated speeches and the need, interest, and values of the audience take a back seat to the business benefit of public speaking.

Audiences make public speaking necessary and are to always be considered when you select your topics. Speakers should choose topics that are relevant to their particular audience as well as important to them, addressing issues that affect their lives, topics that bridge gaps, and confront issues that may alter their future growth. The above-mentioned is successfully done when a speaker approaches the topic knowing who their audience is and what their needs are.

The Occasion

Why am I here? Why are they here? Simple enough? Absolutely! From those two questions we arrive at the occasion. Our topics must be equally appropriate for both the audience and occasion. For instance; if your speech was on a religious holiday, i.e., Easter or Christmas, a political holiday, i.e., Memorial Day, or Independence Day, it would be tailored for that occasion and audience. Some speech occasions are ceremonial in nature, such as a toast at a wedding or anniversary, the presentation or acceptance of an award, or a keynote speaker at a graduation that focuses on the present and positive praise of the individuals. Other speeches are deliberate, meaning the hiring host will assign the speaker the topic, giving them the specifics about the audience and the occasion and the speaker is left to do the appropriate research to tailor the speech for the need of the audience. Also, the occasion will narrow the scope of topic selections too, if you were giving a toast to a friend's new business opening you would not want to refer to the rate of new business failures or mention your new co-worker that had to get a job because his start-up failed; instead you may want to talk about determination, courage, and the commitment it takes to start a new venture. If delivering a eulogy, you would focus on giving positive accolades and achievements of the deceased—not that they had poor eating habits, which probably resulted in their death. These are examples of how the occasion will restrict your topic selections automatically. This would also apply to awareness events like Breast Cancer, AIDS, or American Heart Association. The clues are in the occasion itself.

Consider One's Self

Reflecting back to our scenario when Missy was nervous about her inability to come up with a topic that she felt was of interest to the audience, and decided to get help from her instructor. The instructor asked her some key questions, which resulted in her realizing that she had an amazing family vacation to Haiti that would be a great topic after all.

If your topic is of interest to you and you are enthusiastic when talking about it, chances are it will be of interest to others. Consider what you talk to those that are close to you about, what causes are you passionate about, what social issues make you want to march with a sign, or personal concerns that you are willing to sign a petition for? These along with hobbies, interest, unusual talents, travel, co-cultural affiliations, and employment will be great starts in selecting topics, also when choosing familiar areas it will expedite the topic selection and minimize the amount of research you will have to do.

Granted that familiar subjects are the best way to select a topic, however, an alternative is to choose one that you are interested in knowing more about. Wanting to learn more about something will ignite a spark and will motivate your research and ultimately your delivery of the speech itself.

Brainstorming

This is also a proven method of assisting in selection of a topic; *brainstorming* is a method of shared problem solving in which all members of a group spontaneously contribute ideas. It is also a similar process undertaken by a person to solve a problem by rapidly generating a variety of possible solutions and is used to generate speech topics. The process is to give yourself a time frame of 3–5 minutes, get writing material, and without judgement (which is the first rule of brainstorming) write down whatever comes to mind. Make no attempts

Figure 4.1

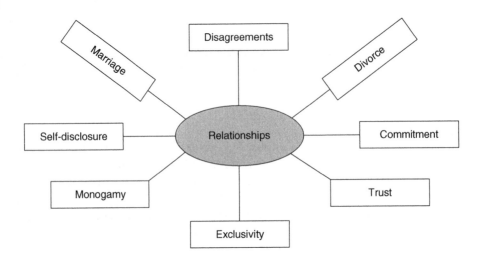

to evaluate if the ideas are good or bad, just focus on writing them down as fast as you can. Allow your mind to think freely as it channels ideas one after the other. This technique can be done independently but is more entertaining with a group of friends, which allows for a larger pool of ideas to choose from.

You may want to incorporate various systems to help your creative juices to flow like using the letter system and the alphabet system; for example, choose one topic beginning with the letter A, two topics beginning with the letter B, and three topics beginning with the letter C and so on. Perhaps you may be a visual thinker, then you can try a technique called *mapping*; this is when your ideas are linked together in a cluster like a spider's web. The idea is to start with a topic or idea in the center, then as ideas related to the topic come to you, write them down around the centered idea, then draw a line to link them together. Even if your ideas seem awkward or simplistic, try not to reject them, wait until all possibilities have been exhausted, continue this until your time is up. When your time is up, you should have quite a list—quantity is key; the longer the list the better chances of selecting a great topic. Use the one not chosen for future reference and assignments.

See Figure 4.1 for example.

4.2 Narrowing Your Topic

Once you have brainstormed and determined your topic, you will now need to narrow it down to something that you will be able to cover thoroughly in the time your instructor has allotted for your speech. Usually the time is somewhere around 4–6 minutes for major speech assignments.

Speech topics many times can be too broad and students can find themselves overwhelmed with too much information. For example, take a topic like "cars"—how would you possibly cover a topic as large as that in 4–6 minutes? You absolutely could not do it, cars is an extremely broad topic and would take weeks to cover it all, no matter how fast you talked.

Nevertheless, there is the process of narrowing the topic to fit into the time you have been given to work with. If you are working with a broad topic such as "cars," you may first choose to break it into categories like:

Cars
Muscle cars
Hot rods
Movie cars
Exotic cars
Antique
Vintage

Now you would still find that this is still too broad and you would still not be able to cover it in your 4–6 minute time frame. However, if you narrow it down to, perhaps, vintage cars, and their enthusiasts in America, the topic would now be narrowed to fit into the allotted time, narrow enough that research is not difficult, but if so there are still others to choose from.

4.3 Available Resource for Researching Topics

Narrowing the topic is great progress, together with research it will make for a well-prepared speech and delivery. Many are the sources for which one gathers research material for their speeches; they include personal experience, internet sources, print source, electronic databases, and interviews.

Personal Experience

As stated earlier in the text, starting with your personal experiences are great starters to finding solid topics, likewise with research. Your personal experience will constitute you as being your very first source . . . research simplified. And it will also aid in avoiding the great temptation to plagiarize because you are already armed with a wealth of knowledge on the subject. These personal experiences could be a unique talent, a skill, international travel, or perhaps an expert of sorts, you may be an award-winning cyclist who has competed around the world, a restorer of classic cars, or served in the armed forces, situations such as these will allow you to incorporate great examples, anecdotes, and illustrations as supporting material as well.

Many personal experiences include family members or friends that relate to the topic, simply write down particular instances that can be used to support your main points. Remember also, that audiences love to hear personal experiences, it adds interest to your topic as well as increases your credibility.

Internet Sources

This is the first choice most student's will seek when a speech topic is to be considered, so it should not surprise anyone that it is the first when the issue of research is at hand. Being that this is true; the main concern should be that the internet research is accurate, current, and objective for your topic. To do well in finding such information you need to know the appropriate search terms, evaluate internet sources, and how to use multiple search engines.

- Appropriate Search Terms—Current books, journal articles from electronic databases are great tools in locating keywords for your topics. For advanced searches, use the wildcard (*) added to various keywords.
- Evaluate Internet Sources—User is responsible for carefully evaluating sources to determine how current, credible, accurate, and unbiased each source is. Compare data found on the internet with one or more print sources. Internet sources are to be equally as accurate as a print reference; they should include the author, date, title of article, website title, and the date site was accessed.
- Multiple Search Engines —These search engines are to search websites on the internet. When researching speech topics use multiple search engines and conduct multiple searches. A list of search engines follows, which you may find useful:
  Google.
  Bing
  Yahoo. . . .
  Baidu. . . .
  AOL. . . .
  Ask.com. . . .
  Excite. . . .
  DuckDuckGo.

Print Sources

Never conduct any research without the use of print sources, which are magazines, books, and newspapers.

- Magazines and Scholarly Journals can be accessed in your campus library or the electronic databases such as EBSCOhost
- Books can be locate at your city or campus library using the online catalog for your topic, a librarian is always available if you should have any problem locating what you need, many libraries offer online chatting with a librarian as well.
- Newspapers are also available in your library, providing current and have up-to-date information; you may also use online newspaper sources like chron.com or nytimes.com

Electronic Databases

Who among us is not a googler? We all are, and it has made research much easier and accessible; however, it can become overwhelming during times of research as there are so many sites. With this in mind, there is Google Scholar, which indexes and locates scholarly articles, however, for a nominal fee unless you utilize the electronic databases already purchased by your campus library. These databases will allow you access to full-text articles at no personal cost to you and is accessible 24/7 from the privacy of your own home or dorm room. There are over 200 but we will only list a few to get you started.

- EBSCOhost (ebscohost.com) serves thousands of libraries and other institutions with premium content in every subject area.
- Ebrary Academic and Public Library Complete
  offers authoritative e-books in a wide range of subject areas, along with powerful tools to help you find, use, and manage the information you need.
  CQ Researcher Online is often the first source that librarians recommend when researchers are seeking original, comprehensive reporting and analysis on issues in the news.
  Ebscohost E-Book Collection searches a multitude of online books and electronically checks them out.

Interviews

When all else fails and you cannot get the answers, you need consider doing a personal interview of someone that has vast knowledge of the subject. People are more eager than you might think to share their experiences with others; even so you must make sure they are regarded as credible to your audience on the topic. If they are not familiar to your audience you can demonstrate such by referring to their credibility by making a brief reference to their relevant background. Here are a few things you should cover when requesting an interview:

- Explain the purpose of the interview
- Schedule the interview, set it at a time that is convenient for the subject
- Plan questions ahead of time
- Send questions ahead for approval
- Set time, only request a reasonable amount of time, do not exceed time and never be late.

4.4 Supporting Material

A good speech should include supporting materials from secondary sources to add, clarification, interest and proof to back up claims made within the speech. Moreover, they add credibility and provide listeners with a way to research more about the topic.

Let's explore several types of supporting material and how they might be used in your efforts to prepare and present an audience centered and compelling speech.

Examples

Case or incidence that represents what the speaker is talking about.

For example, if the speaker was speaking about his prize-winning show car, he would bring pictures of the car at the car show or his trophy standing by the car.

Statistics

Figures that maximize the overall point of the speech, when used adequately it can greatly influence the audience. Note the two examples as follows:

- Not many people in the history or this vintage car show win in this category.
- Less than 2 percent in 30 years of this vintage show competition has won in this category.

The latter illustrates just how low the winning rate is in this category.

Testimony

What's better than a "I saw it with my own eyes!" story? So incorporating testimony will also increase credibility of a speech, this is when you use the opinion of others to support your claim. Examples:

- I tried this diet and I lost 10 pounds in 10 minutes.
- Rogaine made the difference; I no longer have a comb over.
- This tooth whitening gel is phenomenal; my friends no longer call me "Molly McButter!"
- Hooked on Phonics is the best, my son taught me how to read in eight weeks.

It is important to realize that there are different types of testimony that may be utilized in maximizing one's credibility when speaking and they are as follows:

- Expert testimony—The testimony of an expert who is well respected as an authority on the topic.
- Prestige testimony—Using the words of a public figure that the audience respects to make a point.
- Laymen's testimony—The use of stories from common people the audience can relate to. Example: New family just moved to the neighborhood and their new neighbor shares with them that they should always buy bottled water and never drink the city water because it's been known to cause cancer and birth defects.

Illustrations

Everyone loves to hear a great story. If you add well-told illustrations, it will guarantee the success of keeping your audience's attention and will also ensure them remembering key points. An illustration almost always guarantees interest by appealing to audience emotions; it is a story which provides an example of an idea, problem, or issue the speaker is discussing.

Definitions

This is necessary when you explain the meaning of a word, idea, or term that may be unfamiliar to your listeners or that may differ from their usual understanding.

Definitions serve to bring clarity to your audience, but do not serve to add interest to your topic.

Explanations

A statement or account that makes something clear, explains how something is done, making it more understandable by outlining the causes or processes.

When a speaker can effectively use supporting material, it makes listening more enjoyable to the audience and their delivery more effective and memorable.

© g-stockstudio/Shutterstock.com

PART 2

Developing Your Speech

Chapter 5

The People in the Seats—Audience Analysis

Learning Objectives

Exploration in this chapter will allow students to discover:
5.1. Know the Three Types of Audience Analysis (demographics, attitude, and situational)
5.2. Strategies for Effectively Analyzing an Audience
5.3. Strategies for Adapting to Your Audience
5.4. Creating an Audience Profile

© Daniel Lohmer/Shutterstock.com

The audience is undoubtedly the last thing a person thinks about when they see an image like the one at the beginning of this chapter of President Barak Obama delivering the Commencement address at Notre Dame. Most people would only focus on the fact that the president himself was in the image; never taking into consideration the mechanics of what must take place for a speaker to prepare for such a speech. A speaker cannot approach an audience until they know something about them and the situation in which they are to speak.

Each individual audience member brings its own attitudes, belief, values, and expectations to the public speaking event, which in large part is due to their own experiences, and unique cultural background. An audience may be diverse but will still share similar characteristics, and these characteristics are discovered by the skilled speaker who knows that an audience analysis must be done in order to successfully accommodate their audience.

In preparation for the public speaking event of the president's commencement address to Notre Dame these key elements about the audience were essential; who they were, what they believed in, and how to appeal to their sense of values. For the purpose of knowing *the people in the seats* we will unfold various methods and strategies in this chapter to learn how to obtain such information.

We will begin by exploring the three types of audience analysis; they will be divided into three parts: demographic analysis, attitude analysis, and situational analysis. All three are important for you to do, and more than likely speakers will most times start with the most obvious one first—demographic analysis.

5.1 Three Types of Audience Analysis

Demographic Analysis

Assumptions about an audience can easily be made by categorizing them by their demographic makeup. This is considered the statistical characteristics of a group, examples of these statistical characteristics of an audience include:

Race	Political affiliation	Cultural Heritage
Age	Marital status	Sexual orientation
Gender	Parental status	
Education	Geographic location	
Religion	Type of Residence	
Socioeconomic class	Group affiliations	
Occupation	Government Assisted Programs	

These social categories are important; some more than others depending on what your topic is about. They reveal various beliefs and values that audience members may share and would likely affect how they will respond to various topics and speaking styles. In like manner, never neglect to consider the significance of cultural diversities—people from other cultures may have varied perspectives toward the topic. Audience-centered speakers are particularly mindful of this as their primary focus is to be all inclusive, respectful, and culturally sensitive.

© Rawpixel.com/Shutterstock.com

Conducting a demographic analysis would prove relatively easy for your classroom assignments, as you could easily observe age, race, and cultures of your peers. Because of the geographical makeup the majority of you may share the commonality of campus dorm living, work study, social club affiliations, meal plans and/or ramen noodle plans; do not take for granted that all demographic characteristics are visible so waiting until the last minute could be disastrous for a speaker, so get analysis done well in advance perhaps a week before delivering your speech.

For presentations outside of the classroom setting, you should be able to obtain geographic information from the event host, which would be the person close enough to the situation to have access to the information you need about your intended audience members, so ask them as many questions as possible. Never assume anything . . . you know what they say when you "assume" right? Well if not; ask somebody!

Attitude Analysis

An attitude is "a relatively enduring organization of beliefs, feelings, and behavioral tendencies towards socially significant objects, groups, events or symbols" (Hogg & Vaughan 2005, p. 150).

Being that demographic information is significantly important they are but a fraction of analyzing your audience and cannot reveal all you need to know about them; you also need to know what their attitudes are about the topic, purpose, and the speaker and this is acquired through an attitude analysis. Let's break down the three major factors you should consider about your audience's attitudes.

Attitudes toward Your Topic

Attitude—a person's likes or dislikes. It is important to understand that your audience will have a general feeling about your topic. When taking that into consideration you should now think about what degree of interest and knowledge they already have in the topic. If you are speaking to persuade, consider the degree of agreement your audience is with your position on the topic. Next we will examine each of them.

Interested Audience

This aspect is a no brainer, if your topic is relevant and interesting to your audience your task is to simply grab and keep their interest throughout the presentation. This is done by giving accurate and current information on the topic, engaging the audience, and delivering the content enthusiastically. Important to realize, uninterested audience members can become interested if the speaker does a good job and is well prepared with strategies to be audience centered, showing a willingness to meet the needs and consider the values of the entire audience.

Knowledge

Assessing the degree of knowledge your audience has about your topic is quite necessary. If your audience has minimal knowledge about the topic, be mindful never to talk down to them or over their heads but instead implement basic concepts to inform them of the subject matter . . . enthusiastically teach them.

Perhaps you are speaking to an audience that possesses vast knowledge on the topic; then your job is to respond to what the audience already knows about the topic. Moreover, if you have concerns regarding your audience has heard of any of your speaking points before or if they have enough insight on the topic to follow concepts and rational you must still be mindful to be cautious not to overestimate the audience's knowledge of the topic either, intelligence does not mean knowledge, oftentimes speakers will rush through complicated material, avoid using planned visuals or fail at telling the audience things that are relevant or new; leaving audience with the feelings of having wasted their time.

Agreement/Disagreement

In the preparation of persuasive speeches you must conclude from your audiences' demographics for what level of agreement they have with your position. In cases of controversial topics you will have audience members on the opposing side of your position, some may strongly agree while others are neutral. Extensive effort must go into gathering as much information as possible about your audience to make a judgement on where they will range from strongly opposing and strongly agreeing with your position.

Attitude toward Speaker

"So you're the one! I saw your bio, I thought you'd be taller from your photograph, you changed your hair I see, looks different in the picture. Well my colleague told me about when you spoke at this event last year and said I should come out to hear what you had to say so . . . I'm here. Maybe I'll see you after the program."

What does your audience know about you? Does your reputation precede you? Do they already know who you are? What is your background in respect to your topic? Is their attitude toward you favorable or unfavorable?

These questions have everything to do with a speaker's credibility, or ethos. Meaning that your credibility relies upon the audience's perception of your competence, character, and charisma, above all in order for you to be perceived as credible they need to know that you know what you are talking about. The audience must believe that you are a trustworthy speaker, an enthusiastic speaker, knowledgeable and interesting—these are key in fostering a positive perception and credibility from your audience.

A speaker without credibility is like wearing an Armani suit without the pants . . . the most essential element is missing . . . you may as well go home.

A speaker's credibility can be direct, secondary, or indirect. When it is *direct credibility* it is derived from first-hand experience; for example, if you are going to speak about swimming with sharks and you have actually swam with sharks, then you would speak from first-hand experience and are then considered to have credibility.

Secondary credibility is derived when you are citing evidence from others, perhaps an article, book, or an author. Stating for instance, "according to Davis of the Huffington Post, swimming with sharks are among the ten most trending things to achieve on one's bucket list."

Now *indirect credibility* is not one to be taken lightly as it is derived from you actually delivering an effective presentation; the burden of proving you are credible is on you and you alone. Therefore, your work is cut out for you in shaping your audience's attitude toward you, referencing to the short introduction of this segment when the audience member spoke to the speaker about their knowledge of who they were through a colleague. It is obvious that the audience member, however, void of personality found the secondary credibility to be intriguing enough to attend the speaking event of the speaker not to mention, will ensure that the audience member will likely believe what you say and think that you are knowledgeable, interesting, and dynamic.

Attitude toward Being There

This attitude is widely overlooked but is highly important, knowing what an audience's attitude is toward being at a speaking event will allow you to have clear understanding of how best to meet their needs and prepare according to their feelings about being there. Being that your audiences are *voluntary, involuntary,* or *accidental* each one poses their own set of circumstances. Voluntary audiences are just that, they are in attendance because they choose to be. Either it is their feelings about the speaker or the topic. Even the type of event itself would be sufficient reason for many to attend, even to the extent of purchasing tickets to attend. The voluntary audience members may also be there because of their desire to actively participate in the event. With an audience like this the speaker has a greater advantage than when dealing with other types; however, the challenge with this one is the task of fulfilling the expectation of the audience, giving them what they paid for or anticipated hearing or gaining.

You are expected to give speeches is this class because of the requirements of a public speaking course the same is true of some audiences as they form because they are required. For example; an *involuntary audience* are those like this very class; you would prefer not to be here but it is a part of your degree plan so here you are for four and a half months. This is also called a captive audience. Students will be audience members listening to many varying topics, some perhaps controversial, against personal values or downright boring; nevertheless, Dr. So-N-So demands you be in attendance.

Other instances are mirrored in one's professional and social environment such as: required faculty and staff convocations before each semester mandated by the president of the University, required job trainings or continuing education units (CEUs). We see the challenge here is that with class speeches, faculty convocations, and trainings is that people may only be there in "warm body" mode, while having little interest in the topic, open hostility toward speaker and topic, lack of attention or participation.

These situations are unpleasant for both the audience and the speaker; however, it can end with a happy medium. The audience-centered speaker's responsibility is to have knowledge from his or her audience analysis, which will give insight as to why the audience is in attendance and tailor their speech to address those issues and speak ethically, being sensitive and tolerant of differences.

If the speaker purposely addresses the audience with understanding and consideration, the reason they have been asked to listen to you, and being mindful of their time they have a high chance of winning that involuntary audience over.

Addressed now is, the *accidental audience*, the ones that are solicited by speakers or host from people just passing by for whatever reason. This audience is less probable than the others but it is certainly likely to occur on college campuses where many student organizations are trying to make their causes known and recruit members who are like-minded. Also, during political campaigns politicians know that campuses are filled with students who are voting age and they will stop them to talk about issues that may be relevant to students.

Other examples for this type of audience would be: social and environmental activist. The overall challenge with accidental audience is that the persons of whom you are soliciting were on their way somewhere, which means they would be pressed for time and if they did stop you would not have full participation or focus, they would be preoccupied. Oftentimes these audience members will leave after a brief stay thus your intended message was fragmented. These public address systems are seen in high traffic areas, or well-traveled areas like malls, sporting events, or student centers.

Situational Analysis

So far we have focused on the people in the seats, your actual audience, being they voluntary, involuntary, or accidental and the primary concern remains being an audience-centered speaker in spite of the challenges. Equally important, a speaker should also take into consideration the speaking situation. Situational analysis will initially address why there is a need to address your audience. The occasion and circumstances associated with the occasions will determine when the audience should be addressed and will also determine consequences according to the way they are addressed. A case and point: Hurricane Katrina, which destroyed New Orleans in August

© J. Norman Reid/Shutterstock.com

2005; the hurricane struck the Gulf Coast of America devastating large parts of Louisiana, Mississippi, and Alabama; however, the most desperation was in New Orleans. In all, Hurricane Katrina killed nearly 2,000 people and affected some 90,000 square miles of the United States. Hundreds of thousands of evacuees scattered far and wide.

Most compelling evidence of a poor audience analysis of the situation was by government officials in the aftermath of the Hurricane, causing a negative reaction worldwide. Federalism sprang to the forefront in public debates about the response to Hurricane Katrina as officials from the national, state, and local government sought to shift blame to other levels of government (Publius, 2008). The mayor of the city Ray Nagin gave his first warning of the Hurricane only a day before landfall, which gave many people too short a notice to evacuate thus offering the Superdome as a shelter of last resort.

Many people showed acts of heroism, the Coast Guard, rescuing 34,000 people in New Orleans, ordinary citizens offered food and shelter to assist their neighbors; however, the government namely the federal government appeared unprepared for the disaster. The Federal Emergency Management Agency (FEMA) took days to set up operations in New Orleans, seemingly without a concrete plan of relief. Officials including President George W. Bush did not even have clear idea of what catastrophic ruins the hurricane had caused; how much aid, food, and water were needed, how many people were stranded or missing, how many homes and businesses were destroyed.

Katrina had left in her wake one of the most costly natural disasters, as well as one of the five deadliest hurricanes, in the history of the United States and the president waited two days to cut his vacation short to return to the White House to directly engage in relief strategies. Due to this thoughtless response to the victims and public, Americans deemed his presidency over. Headlines read unfavorably to his response then and since, such as: Katrina thrusts race and poverty onto national stage, or The seven worst moments of George W. Bush's presidency. The US Global Leadership Report showed (Gallup) 56 percent was the disapproval rating for him at that time. On September 15, Bush gave a speech in an attempt to repair his image (Benoit & Henson, 2009).

A speaker's knowledge and understanding of situations will serve as their guide during the speech preparation process giving them the tools to properly address the audience needs. Remember also that an audience-centered speaker will know that various occasions hold true to certain expectations and address them accordingly. For instance; the above-mentioned situation would be one to address promptly so those affected would be reassured that provisions for them were a top priority. Likewise, if you were a bridesmaid at your best friend's wedding, the expectation would be to share positive expressions about her and not things that would cause embarrassment for her and the groom. Whatever the occasion is, take the proper time to know and follow proper protocols.

5.2 Strategies of Effectively Analyzing Audiences

Audience attitudes and beliefs can be determined by merely asking them what they think. We will explore the informal and formal strategies of audience analysis in this section, which will provide you with useful and appropriate tool when gathering information about your audience.

The *informal audience analysis* is when you ask a sample of your audience questions concerning your topic, also one of the most effective methods is you can ask the event host or event sponsors. They want nothing more than the success of the event as well as your speech. The speaker can ask such questions as: Who will be in the audience? Why do they want to hear my speech? Are they already familiar with my topic? What do they want or expect to hear? These methods work well when a speaker is unable to conduct a more formal analysis.

Formal audience analysis will take one having resources and will afford you to get more accurate and reliable information that could not be obtained through an informal audience analysis. Listed in the following are ways you may gather information about your audience through formal analysis.

Focus Groups

These consist of small groups of people randomly selected from members of your actual audience or similar group. Group size is usually 8–12 members with similar demographic and socioeconomic characteristics such as all women or teens but will have a range of varying views. The discussion should last 90 minutes to 2 hours.

Questionnaires

The second formal strategy is the questionnaire; it is designed for you to obtain demographics and attitude analysis. The questions should be carefully planned, being clear, specific, straightforward, and objective. Questionnaires can be administered either over the phone or in person. The self-report is the best known form of questioning as it is a list of questions members are given and asked to complete in writing. Figure 5.1 presents a sample Audience Analysis Form.

Figure 5.1 Audience Analysis Form
Audience Analysis Form

This instrument can be used to gather information by phone, in person, or through e-mail

Demographic Analysis

_____ % Men; _____ % Women; _____ % Married _____ % Living Together _____ % with Children

Number in each age group: _____ 17–20; _____ 21–25; _____ 26–30; _____ 31+

Religious Preference or Background _____

Primary Co-Culture Background _____

Educational Background (indicate highest degree earned) _____

Are you employed? _____

Annual Salary (if minor, parents' annual salary) _____

Current Marital Status _____

Where do you live? _____

How many children do you have? _____

Attitude Analysis

1. Attitude toward topic

Interest in topic: _____ interested _____ uninterested _____ neutral

Knowledge of topic _____ good _____ fair _____ poor

Agreement with topic: _____ strongly agree _____ Agree _____ Neutral _____ Disagree

_____ Strongly disagree

2. Attitude toward speaker

Attitude toward me: _____ positive _____ negative _____ neutral

3. Attitude toward attendance: _____ Voluntary _____ Involuntary _____ Accidental

Situational Analysis:

Number of people expected to attend: 10–20 _____ 21–30 _____ 31–40 _____ 40+

Maximum time allotted for speech: _____ Preferred length _____

Room Setup: _____ Audience in chairs _____ Audience at tables _____ Speaker on stage _____

_____ Speaker on level with audience

Equipment available: _____ Lectern/Podium _____ IPad, Tablet, Laptop _____ Microphone

_____ Presenter remote _____ Wi Fi _____

Q& A expected: _____ Yes _____ No

Questions audience may have about topic: _____

_____

Ways topic will impact audience: _____

5.3 Strategies for Adapting to Your Audience

Now that your audience has been identified and sufficient information has been obtained to formulate an innovative audience analysis, you are now prepared to think of ways you may be able to adapt to your audience. Audience adaptation is the process by which a speaker adjusts his topic, purpose, language, and communication style to avoid offending or alienating members of audience and to increase the likelihood of speech goals.

Adapting the Message to the Audience during Preparation

A speaker can use information about the audience to adapt their speech to the particular audience while preparing the speech.

The use of demographic information will assist the speaker's anticipation of the audience and imagine how they will respond to specific aspects to the speech. In the process of structuring the message and keeping the audience in mind a speaker should consider certain aspects to be able to adapt the message:

- What experiences or events he and the audience share and the ways the speaker and the audience are similar. Knowing this will ensure that the speaker meets the audience on common ground as well as identify with them.
- Speaker should use the right words and style of expression, being sure the use of words that the audience can understand; this is referred to as *diction*.
- Speaker should consider examples or analogies that can be used that the audience is likely to find familiar; analogies involve the linking of the unknown to the familiar.
- A speaker should be aware of specialized language or jargon. For example, the language of your particular work, i.e., coach or medical professional may not be familiar to math teacher and would be considered rude as it would exclude them from the conversation/topic and foster feelings of being left out.
- Speaker is responsible for any needed modifications to their speech that may be perceived as negative to the audience before delivering it.
- If the speaker and/or any audience member are from a different culture, be mindful to use phrases that are familiar to ensure understanding for the audience.

Adapting the Message While Delivering the Speech

It is imperative for a speaker to plan to adapt during the speech. With a face-to-face audience in a small room, it is easier for the speaker to observe nonverbal reactions such as looks of confusion or expressions of agreement or disagreement, of frustration or anger and adjust the message accordingly.

An audience-centered speaker is constantly aware of their audience members while speaking. Through eye contact they can read the faces and observe body language to know immediately if an adjustment in necessary; however, this does not mean that a speaker should abandon their views and values and say whatever the audience wants to hear to get their desired outcome either. This would be considered an unethical speaker as opposed to an audience-centered one. Adaptations can be made during a speech by:

- Encouraging the audience to ask questions during the speech.
- If Wi-Fi is available in the speaking location, an audience response system (ARS) or clicker can be used to determine what their opinions are and what they understand about the topic from their notebooks, laptops, or other handheld device and speaker can display response on a screen while speaking and adapt the message accordingly. This tool is useful; however, it can be a bit distracting while typing and could create long pauses without dialogue and could drum up anxiety for the speaker and boredom for the audience.

- Cellphone-enabled response systems such as SMS (short message service) response system can be used as well. They are able to take text input from audience members and receive multiple responses to questions via SMS.
- Many speaking events will have a hashtag that is unique to the presentation or occasion and audience members can send tweets, using their smartphones, and the speaker can respond to the tweets or adapt his or her message in real time. This is also beneficial if displayed as part of a back channel from remote audiences or member of large audiences.

5.4 Creating an Audience Profile

The data gathered from your informal audience analysis, focus group interviews, and questionnaires has now positioned you to develop a well-detailed audience profile. This type of profile will provide the most accurate picture of an audience in varying way that a mere demographic analysis cannot.

Every solid audience profile starts with a fundamental understanding of who your audience is (see Figure 5.2). Demographic profiles are limited in their potential to uncover motivations and patterns. But they're a great launch point for any discussion (De Mers, 2013).

What your audience profile helps you to obtain is a more in-depth knowledge of who your audience is, how they live their lives, to dig deeper into their needs and motivations.

Once you can determine what their most pressing needs, interests, issues, and desires are, you will have easily acquired an invitation into their lives and better know how to tailor a message suitable for your audience. There are two perspectives to consider once this has been achieved;

1. Understanding what influenced your audience to attend your speaking event will allow you to have insight into what methods and strategies to use the next time you are going to speak, it will help you recognize those same influences in others and will also help you in creating more powerful content that will attract more of those type of listeners.
2. A broader understanding of what is driving people to seek out services like yours, which will expand your arsenal of topics, approaches, and more.

Figure 5.2 Audience Profile

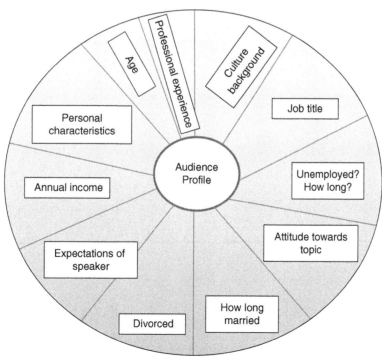

Chapter 6

Verbal Communication

Learning Objectives

Exploration in this chapter will allow students to discover:

6.1. Language Defined and Rules That Govern Its Use
6.2. The Taste of Foot
6.3. Identifying Obstacles of Effective Verbal Communication
6.4. The Power of Language in Society
6.5. Verbal Strategies to Promote Messages Audiences Understand
6.6. Language That Fosters Inclusion Rather Than Alienating Audiences

© JStone/Shutterstock.com

*Words have color, depth, texture of their own, and power to evoke vastly more than they mean;
words can be used to make things clear, make things vivid, make things interesting, and make
things happen inside the one who reads them or hears them."*

— Frederick Buechner

Chelsea angrily enters her home, throws her car keys onto the table, and plops down on the couch next to her mother Michelle. "Nothing agitates me more than a person who refuses to speak directly to me if they have an issue with me personally!" Chelsea yelled. "What is going on and why are you so upset?" inquired Michelle. "For the past couple of days Brett has been either avoiding me or being unusually evasive when we speak on the phone, if I have done something wrong he should tell me, this is upsetting and certainly no way to treat your best friend," Chelsea explained. "I am sorry that the two of you are having trouble, but you have been friends for a long time and I am certain there is a valid reason for his behavior. Situations like this among friends are delicate when we do not fully understand the circumstances so be mindful of what you say," her mother replied.

"Well it may be too late for that because when I insisted on him telling me what was wrong, he kept saying that he just had a lot of things to work through and it had nothing to do with me, which angered me further and I said some horrible things that provoked him to say, "If that is truly the way you feel then perhaps we should re-evaluate our friendship". I wish I would have talked to you about this sooner; it would have made me approach the matter differently and avoided the regret I feel right now," she cried.

© Olena Yakobchuk/Shutterstock.com

"Always understand that even friends go through things that are not for sharing at the moment, there is a time for processing privately, and it is not an indictment against you or the friendship. Allow him some time, and be prepared with an apology and a newfound understanding. Remember; always taste your words before you spit them out," offered Michelle.

As you explore this chapter challenge yourself to identify Chelsea and Brett's verbal communication issues in the opening scenario and what communication encoders could be used to improve their communication skills.

Several verbal communication problems may be identified in our opening scenario, and as we learn what language is and how it is to be used; we hope that through this chapter learners will adapt the ability to use language in ways that are communicatively effective and appropriate as they interact on a daily basis in their work, socially and personally.

Many things that we say without hesitation are out of habit but are not necessarily accurate; some derive from our upbringing, some things we adapt from our surroundings or environment and others are a part of our culture. Every communicative transaction is based on something so familiar and natural to our daily existence like eating, walking, and breathing, yet we rarely take the time to define; it is the remarkable wonder that is language. Quintilian said it best of God having impressed man with no character so proper to distinguish him from other animals, as by the faculty of speech.

6.1 Defining Language, Verbal Communication, and Writing Systems

A little housekeeping is necessary to get a clear pathway to the dining area; let's begin by defining a few terms and acquire a clear path to understanding the familiar albeit important definition of *language*, which is spoken or written words of a particular kind, a means of expressing ideas or feelings or a formal system of signs and symbols that is used to carry information such as sign language. Language is also for the most part a formally established collection of symbols having meaning for a specific group of people, *verbal communication*, however, refers to the use of sounds and language to relay a message, and acts as the primary tool for expression between two or more people. A single verbal symbol is referred to as a *word*, which is a phonetically distinct unit of speech or series of speech sounds that are combined into a single unit producing an assigned meaning. The majority of languages have a distinct formal writing system and there are 14 in use today and can be classified according to the type of sound units the symbols represent; however, we will briefly discuss only a few of them in this chapter.

There are the two basic types: the first is *syllabary* in which all or most of the graphemes represent entire syllables of sound and the first syllabaries were used by Chinese, Egyptians, Mexican, Japanese, Samaritan, and Cherokee cultures.

The second type of writing system is the *alphabet*, where each of the graphemes represents or mostly represents single sounds rather than entire syllables. Today alphabets are the most widespread type of writing in use. As it is interesting and important that writing systems are in association with language, it is equally important to know that one has to be taught a writing system to understand it and acquire the ability to use it, and many below a certain education level are incapable of comprehending written language entirely. Unlike written language, humans can naturally acquire fluent spoken language without being taught. Each human group ever encountered possesses its spoken language.

Symbolism of Language

Having a basic knowledge of what language, verbal communication, and writing systems are has us abreast of why we have our broad vocabulary that is suitable for engaging one another during daily interactions; we now must understand why language is symbolic. Our language differs one from another and while the words we use are unique to us, they may differ from someone else's. Misunderstandings are common among varying cultures when it comes to language—why else do we purchase a dictionary or download an app when we travel abroad, to have an understanding of their unique symbols? Language is a symbol or testament of one's culture. Commonly, however, when someone misunderstands what we say, we are quick to refer to the dictionary and get the *denotative meaning*—which is merely the dictionary's literal definition—to verify the proper use of the word. However, the emotions and associations connected to a word are known as its *connotative meaning*. Depending on our experiences, certain words have a positive, negative, or neutral connotation. Moreover, words do not have meaning unless we assign meaning to them; many words are the same but the meanings are different according to the meaning we associate with them; listed below are some examples:

The Word	Denotative Meaning	Connotative Meaning
Bad	Unsatisfactory	Somethings exceptionally great "she's bad"
Dog	K-9, Animal	Term of endearment "that's my dog"
Bitch	Female dog	Derogatory term for women or weakness in men
Coke	Soft drink	Illegal drug
Queen	Female Ruler	Reference to a gay male
Nigga	Racial slur	Homie, bro, brother, term of endearment (Sentiment not shared by all)
Hoe	Garden tool	Promiscuous male or female
Hot	High degree of heat	Reference to an attractive man or woman

The above-mentioned examples are clear evidence that language is *symbolic* and words don't mean unless people assign them meaning, they are mere symbols that represent ideas, feelings, objects, or events in our experience. Something important to share is that when people respond to words they are responding to the connotative meaning, not the denotative meaning. Equally important to share is that you should realize that even when you think you are using commonly understood terms, the chances are great that you and your communication partner may not share the exact meaning.

Language and Culture

Knowing now of language and symbols and how words are formed as well as how they may be the same but are assigned meaning by a culture, we will now learn further the magnitude of importance of language and culture, and how one's frame of reference is significantly a product of them.

We learned about frame of reference earlier in Chapter 1 of the text and how it affects how we use language in the communication process. For a broader understanding of this, we will discuss people from high-context cultures and how their expectations differ about verbal encoding than those of people from low-context cultures. *High-context cultures* are those that primarily use nonverbal methods to relay meaningful information in conversation such as eye movement, facial expression, and tone of voice. In these cultures the situation, people, and nonverbal elements are more important than the actual words communicated, as a result they are many times vulnerable to communication breakdowns, more so with diverse members as they assume more shared understanding than really exist.

People from high-context cultures include countries like Japan, Brazil, Native American tribal groups including most countries located in Africa, as well as the majority of the Middle East including Iraq and Iran. They tend to encode messages in a less direct manner, always concerned about not to offend the listener with expressions that are blunt or harsh.

Conversely, people of *low-context cultures* are those with whom you can expect things to be concisely spelled out, they are direct and to the point. Considerable dependence is on what is said or written

© imtmphoto/Shutterstock.com

and more responsibility is placed on the listener to keep up their knowledge base; they "shoot from the hip" so to speak. Their explicitness in communicating can often cause offence and resentment. These low-context cultures include Germany, Norway, Denmark, Sweden, Finland, Canada, and the United States.

The nature of business

In addition to communication symbols in language and culture, it is essential that we explore briefly the nature of business among high-context and low-context cultures. In a high-context culture it may take time to build a relationship before your international business partner feels comfortable in talking about business dealings. Meetings of business are more conducive if one has been introduced by someone who knows you and the other parties of interest and may take a few hours; however, if you present yourself without representation or a "go between" to tell who you are, it could take months, even years, to gain the trust of your international colleagues before they would consider discussions of business or you closing a deal.

Consequently, if you are in the first situation having an introduction and you are negotiating a business deal internationally, this knowledge is imperative. In a high-context culture, a contract is just a starting point

© Niyazz/Shutterstock.com

for negotiations in closing a deal. Signing the contract does not represent a closing of the business deal (Minor & Lamberton, 2010).

In contrast, a written agreement can be taken at face value in a low-context culture. A contract, for example, means exactly what it says, no more and no less than that. A contract is considered the final product of negotiations, not the starting point.

One key thing to remember is high-context cultures are focused on the social context or social environment being more important than the words being spoken (Minor & Lamberton, 2010). Intercultural Communication expert Ray Ruiz tells us, "Countries in Latin American and Asia value the building of relationships all things must work in order to achieve desired goals in business relations between high- and low-context culture.

The point, of course, is that in an age of diversity these cultural differences are just as likely to appear across a desk as they are across borders. Don't assume a common geographic location guarantees a common heritage (Rutledge, 2011).

Language and Gender

Is this really necessary? I mean to talk about language and gender, how does this factor into anything useful in the study of language? Both of them talk that's common knowledge, they do that a lot most times too much and too loud. . . what else is there?

Believe me there is plenty in the grand scheme of things; men and women are also apt to differ in the way they use language verbally. Why else would renowned author John Gray write the book "Women Are from Venus Men Are from Mars?" Low-context and high-context is not only reserved for cultural difference, it is applicable to gender as well. Women are more high-context than men in that they need to be vocal, expressive, and involved from the inception to completion of a situation, their communication goals differ from men.

Women want to keep situations peaceful, a constant line of open communication, monitor everyone's commitment, response, and follow through on the issues whereas men are more task-driven, discuss something initially, give input and or solutions and expect resolutions without constantly coddling the situation. Being aware of these differences it is easy to see how gender and culture play a large role in verbal misunderstanding.

The Rules of Language

Language is ordered into five systems of rules. Whether it is your native language or fluency of a second language, the adaptation of the rules of that language system is essential. Language is rule-governed; it is not haphazard or chaotic, and the rules of a language are highly resistant to change. We will attempt to make explicit some of these rules below.

Phonology

There are varied origins of language across the globe and are all comprised of basic sounds, the sound system of a language is called phonology, which includes the sounds used in that language and how they are combined.

Morphology

This is the system of how words are formed or not formed in a language. The understanding of morphology is associated with the understanding of a morpheme, which is the minimal unit of meaning in a language. These units together create meaning in our language and indicate to us context and tense. Some morphemes that are used will often include prefixes, suffixes, and compound words. It is the individual languages that determine what morphemes can be combined to create words and meaning and the ability to decide that some combinations do not make logical sense.

Syntax

To know grammar is to know syntax. Syntax is the rule of grammar that determines word order, word placement, and word combinations. For example, we would not state that "The chocolate cake eat I did." Syntax tells us that the chocolate cake was not the object eating, and that straightening out the word order will give us the proper meaning. Moreover, proper syntax varies from language to language and learners of other languages often have their work cut out for them learning a new rule of syntax.

Semantics

When speaking of the language rule system of *semantics*, it is the reference of the actual meaning of the words and sentences we are communicating. Every word of a language has a meaning associated with it and the meaning determines how the word is used when communicated. Words can also have more than one semantic meaning in a language, like the words "dog" and "puppy." Both words denote the same kind of animal, and difference in appearances. However, there are also semantic differences between the two words, including size and ages.

Pragmatics

The other rule systems teach us how to create meaning through the use of phonemes, morphemes, word order, and word meaning; however, the fifth and final rule, pragmatics, takes us a step further to adjust our language to fit certain social context in our culture. Pragmatics delves into the complex realm of consciously tailoring our conversation to the people we are communicating with, using figurative language. An example of the use of pragmatics on a daily basis is when we consciously formalize our greetings and small talk when approaching our elders, supervisors, or even our parents as opposed to people our own age, co-workers, or siblings.

6.2 The Taste of Foot

Your insight and understanding of language and the rules that govern languages should prepare you for proper verbal communication transactions in everyday life, socially, personally, and in business. But for many this does not always mean that best practices will be used, often we witness on a personal basis as well as publicly how people just cannot seem to prevent having their toes tickle the roofs of their mouths.

The familiar idiom "put your foot in your mouth" reigns supreme in our society; this is when a person says something that offends, upsets, or embarrasses someone else; moreover, a more consequential manner is when the thing you said usually gets you into trouble, especially if you had not thought carefully before speaking.

© pathdoc/Shutterstock.com

Verbal Communication is powerful, equally are the consequences! For when it goes wrong. . . you have acquired a taste for foot. Below are some nationally known instances:

- Robert Durst, heir to a New York real estate fortune, suspected of the deaths of three people which includes his wife Kathleen, his close friend and journalist Susan Berman, and a neighbor. During the finale of a six-part documentary, Durst is heard mumbling to himself after he leaves an on-camera interview to use the restroom, his lapel microphone still "live." "What the hell did I do?" he asks himself. "Killed 'em all of course," he answers.
- Donald Sterling, former owner of the LA Clippers professional basketball franchise from 1981 to 2014, was secretly recorded by his mistress during a conversation where he told her not to bring black people—including Hall of Famer Magic Johnson—to his games. "It bothers me a lot that you want to broadcast that you're associating with black people." "Do you have to?"
- Cincinnati Bengals head coach Marvin Lewis was being interviewed about the game on a local radio station when the host asked him about how the team might prepare for athletic rookie quarterback Johnny Manziel who at 6″ is considered short for a pro passer. Lewis responded: "You gotta go defend the offense. You don't defend the player. . . Particularly a midget."
- Popular television host, Wendy Williams, sparked outrage after her comments about Historically Black Colleges and Universities (HBCUs), and the NAACP, went viral. Williams made a statement that set proud products of HBCUs off.
  She said. "I would be really offended if there was a school that was known as a historically white college. We have historically black colleges. What if there was the National Organization for White People, only? There's the NAACP. By the way, what is the 'C' for? Colored? Are we still using colored?"
  The comments didn't stop there. Williams then pin-pointed HBCUs even more by saying: "National speeches like this will always rub people the wrong way just like white people will be offended because Spelman College is a historically black college for women. You might feel funny about that. I know I'd feel funny, like I just told you. If there was a white college or whatever." (Laster, 2016)
- Australian-American actor and filmmaker Mel Gibson shocked the world when his racial and violent tendencies were revealed at a traffic stop in 2006 for DUI when he said to a police officer "F*cking Jews. . . the Jews are responsible for all the wars in the world." Then in 2010 an audio tape of him threatening to kill his girlfriend during a heated argument, as the feud ignited she tells Mel, "You're gonna answer one day, boy, you're gonna answer."
  Infuriated, Mel asks if she is threatening him, her reply: "I'm not the one to threaten."
  And that's when Mel makes what certainly can be interpreted as a death threat, telling her: "Threaten ya? I'll put you in a f*ckin rose garden you c*nt! You understand that? Because I'm capable of it. You understand that?"
- March 23, 2010, Vice-President Joe Biden, who is known for his humor and gaffes, had a blunder while his microphone was still open. After introducing President Obama at the health care bill signing ceremony, he turned to him with his mic barely off and said, "This is a big F*cking deal." This is said to have been his blue collar way of saying "a job well done." Biden is fondly known for his reputation of saying the wrong thing at the wrong time, there is even a list called the "Top 10 List of Joe Biden Gaffes."

It is clear to see that if one's verbal communication is not controlled, there could be extenuating consequences; the taste of foot comes in many flavors as the above-mentioned situations prove. The taste of foot for Robert Durst tasted like an indictment from the FBI for murder; for Don Sterling a lifetime ban from the NBA; for Marvin Lewis a firestorm among fans and a large helping of humble pie during his public apology; for Wendy Williams a gross backlash from African American HBCU alum, fans attempting to boycott her show, and the loss of her sponsorship with Chevrolet; Mel Gibson's foot chews yielded him rejection by the public, blacklisted in Hollywood, and dropped by his talent agent in 2010; and as for Vice-President Joe Biden, well he has endearingly been said to have the "foot in mouth disease" and having his own list of his most humorous moment as well as gaffes.

To anyone who has the ability to speak this could be you, the spoken word is powerful and must be handled responsibly and with mindfulness, for the lack thereof will cause you to bear personal witness to "the taste of foot."

6.3 Identifying Obstacles of Effective Communication

Effective communication occurs when someone's intended meaning successfully and accurately reaches another person. Yet problems can occur at many junctures, from the initial sender using the wrong language or medium, through noise or interruptions to the message along the way, up to the receiver misinterpreting the message. Potential obstacles to effective communication arise on several levels, from individual to organizational; we will discuss some precautions to prevent the worst of these obstacles.

Individual Impediments

Communication obstacles start individually as each person's emotional and mental situation is different, thus the way we understand messages when received differ as well. Consider a letter being sent with the same content to two individuals, when it is read both will pick up opposite interpretations. Your preconceived notions about a person can also affect the outcome of communication transactions. If you have feelings that the sender is dishonest, you will not believe the message. Also, when you are fearful and vulnerable, this will cause you to suppress or withdraw the intended message.

Poor Encoding

Poor Encoding takes place when the sender/source fails to create the right sensory stimuli to meet the objectives of the message. For instance, in person-to-person communication, verbally phrasing words poorly so the intended communication is not what is actually meant is the result of poor encoding. Also, differences due to translation or cultural understanding can result in the message receiver having a different frame of reference for how to interpret words, symbols, and sounds.

Poor Decoding

This refers to a message receiver's error in processing the message so that the meaning given to the received message is not what the source intended. Again, as we noted above, if the receiver's frame of reference is different (e.g., meaning of words are different) then decoding problems can occur.

Interpersonal Complications

The second two or more people come together to communicate the possibility for obstacles can occur. Differences may compound, personalities can clash, and understandings differ according to a cultures interpretation no matter what content or channel they use.

Physical Barriers

Even the physical structure can block communications. People many times need physical closeness to discuss work problems and share solutions. Oftentimes this works against rather than for the parties in that some people need and require their space and are easily annoyed by close proximity. More than wanting one's space, this separation is intentionally used to avoid communicating altogether. In personal relations closed doors tell partners and friends that you don't want to be bothered with them, in the workplace it indicates that colleagues or managers are too busy to talk. Separations with doors, walls, or a large space hinder the communication process.

Medium Failure

Sometimes communication channels break down and end up sending out weak or faltering signals. "Can you hear me now?" This phrase is used constantly when communicating via cellphone, as this medium has the tendency to fail frequently. Important emails get lost in our junk folder. Other times the wrong medium is used to communicate the message. For example, trying to teach medical professionals a new groundbreaking procedure for heart transplants with a PowerPoint presentation with only pictures, would be an epic failure as this would be more effective with a video showing the procedure actually being performed accompanied by print, which would allow doctors to take their time evaluating the information.

Communication Noise

Noise in communication occurs when an outside force in some way affects delivery of the message. The most obvious example is when loud sounds block the receiver's ability to hear a message. Nearly any distraction to the sender or the receiver can lead to communication noise.

Jargon

When you are involved in a communication transaction, be mindful of using over-complicated, unfamiliar, and technical terms as this is a common barrier to effective communication. Jargon is acceptable in one's profession and co-culture groups as it expedites their communication process in meetings and at work. However, in different settings this jargon could bring the communication to a standstill, as this would seem like a foreign language to them. Talking over someone else's head using terms that they do not know is considered unprofessional and rude and can cause misunderstanding or no understanding at all. Terms that are specific to your work, culture, hobbies, and interest should be avoided when a lay person is present.

Physical Disabilities

Physical disabilities such as hearing problems or speech difficulties are common obstacles to communication.

Language Differences

Due to societal diversity, the many language differences we deal with on a daily basis are common in the breakdown in how we communicate with each other, not only the language but it is also unfamiliar accents, even when the language for the same understanding is still limited.

Trigger Words

Being aware of trigger words provides the opportunity to use different words that will lead to more positive communication outcomes. The proverbial "We need to talk," "We have a problem," "Are you sitting down?," "I heard something today," "Well let me see your phone then" are words that trigger the receiver and their thoughts are immediate in thinking that the conversation is guaranteed to be negative. Also, these could cause different feelings according to how well you know a person, and their frame of reference. Use of these trigger words or language choices can stir up internal psychological noise in the receiver.

Sexist language is another example of verbal encoding that can trigger some intense emotions. Using pronouns that exclude either gender is still common in our society in spite of decades of efforts in feminist consciousness-raising. Gender-specific titles and pronouns can subtly influence sexism as well as our thoughts and expectations about gender roles and appropriate occupations and goals for the sexes. This also include using the word *man* to describe humanity, or even when describing certain professions like fireman, policemen, congressman, spokesmen, clergymen, all are exclusionary of women. Whereas, each of these professions are also performed by capable females but have meant that many would not pursue such profession as they were male-driven. Now these terms have been modified in recent years to firefighter, police officer, congresswoman, spokesperson, or just clergy. Certain professions were also deemed only for a specific gender such as nurses, sports commentators, and engineers. Sexist language is exclusionist, promotes discrimination, and also promotes gender bias.

Racist Language

No matter what your ethnicity is, it is safe to say that you would not appreciate language that implies that you are inferior in intellect, ability, or character to someone else. Unfortunately, every culture has derogatory terms associated with it that others have tagged to it when they desire to be insulting and hurtful. Effective communication is nonexistent when the source engages in racist language, in fact the emotions and/or reactions to such language can most of the times incite behaviors and responses that are injurious in nature. Racist language is certainly an obstacle to effective communication and should be avoided.

As you see, many are the obstacles of effective communication and still the list is incomplete; when we are concerned about meeting our desired communication goals these obstacles should be considered. Can you recall times when the above-mentioned obstacles have created unfavorable outcomes in efforts to communicate effectively?

6.4 The Power of Language in Society

Language is the heartbeat of the world as we know it. It is survival, creation, and civilization. Language is an absolute essential to every human being, from each one's inception it was how our parents passed ways of thinking and conversing to their offspring. Language is an accumulation of knowledge, as we learned everything from somebody through language. It is the most powerful tool in human communication; it establishes relationships among friends, as well as allies between countries.

Society would have to re-create itself every generation if it could not pass its knowledge on through language. Language fuels our aspirations, desires, and creativity; it is what is used to allow us to evolve our ideas and beliefs into reality.

When we think of the power of language in our society, we can certainly associate its use in government, which shapes the way citizens function throughout daily matters of life. Our three branches of government, executive, legislature, and judiciary, all use the power of language to create laws, carry them out, and evaluate them.

Executing laws that directly impact the lives of citizens would not be possible if not for language.

From every natural disaster, public discourse, or public health concern, we expect to hear an announcement or address from officials to give insight, comfort, and solutions. The power of language is always going to be vital to the way we maneuver in society, it is what is expected and it is what we know to be the most acceptable and effective power in our society.

6.5 Verbal Strategies to Promote Messages Audiences Understand

If the most important part of any speech preparation is the audience, so much is required to be said about audience's understanding of the message. The audience will be hearing you for the first time and you will have limited time to be sure that your message and concepts are clear to them once your speech is over. Here are some strategies to assist you in preparing messages that your audience will understand.

Concentrate on the Core

Remember what your main points are, your specific purpose of what you want your audience to walk away with. Keep it simple and to the point, communicating your key message briefly in clear, straightforward language to ensure your audience will grasp the ideas and retain what is said.

Fluff-Free Speech

Fluffing is for pillows, not speeches; for the speaker who really has something to say, fluffing is not necessary. Fluffing is when speakers use content-free speech, in other words saying a whole lot but saying nothing, also known as bloated speech. It is also what many politician resort to when avoiding answering difficult or embarrassing questions. When writing avoid using these figures of speech:

Metaphors, example: "the curtain of darkness";
Similes, example: "cute as a button";
Cliché's, example: "avoid it like the plague."

Also, to promote understanding steer away from the use of big words in speech and long words when writing when small and short ones will do. As said by Winston Churchill, "Simplicity does not equal simplistic."

Proper Pronunciation

Don't write it if you can't say it! There is nothing more frustrating to sit in an audience and hear someone say "I hope I pronounce this right" from their own speech or just flat out butcher words. This is clear evidence that you did not practice or research prior to your presentation for accuracy or possible revisions.

Speakers should refer to a dictionary or an expert to learn how to pronounce difficult words if they must be used. Moreover, make a special effort to learn how to accurately pronounce the names of key sources or individuals in the audience of whom you will need to refer during your speech. If you have the opportunity, ask individuals directly for the correct pronunciation of their names, and ask someone or consult media sources for accuracy of cities and countries. Remember an audience will become frustrated even defensive when they realize that a speaker hasn't taken the time to learn how to accurately pronounce their names or the cities and state they are from. Mispronounced words to an audience will be perceived as the speaker lacking credibility.

Limited Jargon and Acronyms

Limited here means that the occasional use of technical terms that are unique to a specific group or profession can assure your audience that you are competent on the subject and know what you are talking about, but are to be used only when necessary.

Also, use acronyms, which are words formed from the first letters of each word in a name or phrase. This method simplifies things, for instance to use the acronym NABJ to refer to the National Association of Black Journalist—especially if you will refer to it repeatedly in your speech. Remember to define the acronym quickly, never assume your audience already understands its meaning, and then proceed. Be mindful, that excessive use of both jargon and acronyms will exhaust your audience, therefore moderation is key.

Audiences' Response to Accents and Dialects

Something we all have in common are accents and dialects. Speakers must take theirs into consideration to ensure audiences understand their message. *Accents* are the distinctive way of pronouncing words and are usually determined by the speaker's region or cultural background or native language. Consider the Texan with their southern drawl or the native "Who Dat" of New Orleans who is likely to pronounce their hometown "Nawlins" or New Or-luhns."

Equally, *dialects* too are based on an individual's regional or cultural background but reflect the vocabulary and syntax as well as distinctive accents. Many times speakers are judged unfairly due to their regional and ethnic accents and dialects as they are associated with the speaker level of intellect, status, and credibility. Honestly, one has nothing to do with the other. This is a form of discrimination; it even exists among teachers against students who have foreign accents who label them with learning disabilities thus placing them in remedial classes. This behavior instills separation, insecurities, and feelings of inadequacies in students as the teacher has determined the student as limited and incapable of learning, instead of admitting they are limited in ability and tolerance to teach a student who is different from what they are accustomed to.

Speakers and audiences alike should demonstrate tolerance and respect for others' unique way of communicating, and when it comes to speakers, it should never be expected of you to abandon your own dialect and accent to adapt to the speaking style of your audience as your dialect and accent represent who you are as a person and speaker. However, as a speaker we have a responsibility to our audience to ensure they understand our message and in order to do so adhere to these tips:

- Speak slower so audience members can adjust to your accent, words, and phrase choices.
- Make clear any meanings of the words you use that are dialect-specific, even spelling them out if need be.
- Notice your audiences' nonverbal cues of confusion or misunderstanding and address them promptly (Does everyone understand?).
- Use a phrase from your audiences' dialect and accent as a demonstration of your respect for them.
- Translate when you must rely on phrases from your native language, promoting greater understanding and appreciation for you as a speaker.

6.6 Language That Fosters Inclusion Rather Than Alienating Audiences

Inclusion of your audience in your communication efforts has been stressed throughout this text because it is of great importance. We are going to discuçss language that will help speakers avoid alienating their audiences.

Language to Engage

Every speaker's goal should be to connect to their audience and this is accomplished if a speaker uses language that will engage and empower audiences. Understanding the event, occasion, and who's in the seats, speakers can properly prepare their talking points and strategically interject those messages of inspiration and hope, phrases that are relevant to the needs of the audience. This will tell your listeners that you took time and special interest in them.

Lose the Lame Labels

To speak inclusively it is important to use names or labels that people use for themselves. Our everyday language consists of using labels that may be grossly offensive to individuals and groups but are common to hear. Examples of such labels include:

- Fat people
- Homosexual
- Lesbian
- Retard
- Midget
- Old people
- Mexican
- Dysfunctional home
- Wheelchair bound
- Handicapped
- Poor
- Crackhead
- Colored People/ People of Color

Mindful speakers are cautious of this and will exert the necessary energy to avoid unacceptable labels when addressing individuals and specific groups.

Masculine and Feminine Language

Masculine pronouns should not be used as generic terms for both male and female.
Example: Can everyone take out his journal to record next week's assignment?
    This implies that the group is all male; however, it is majority female. In like manner, refrain from using "man," "men," or "mankind" when you mean "people," women," "men," or "human being."
    Correct Example: Can everyone take out their journals to record next week's assignment?

No Cussing, No Fussing

Inserting profanity in a speech is a mistake! Swear words, dirty jokes, sexist or ethnic jokes, as well as any obscene gestures are always inappropriate as some audience members may find them offensive and the speaker's goal of attempting humor would backfire. Also, profanity goes beyond your poor choice of words, it is also showing disrespect or contempt toward something that others hold sacred, such as religion or negatively mocking a culture, i.e., "black face."
    Some speakers use their platform to vent and it is perceived a fussing at their audience members, being neutral is a skill that all speakers need to hone; remember you are there to meet the needs of your audience. . .whose need is it to pay to get fussed at? They can get that for free.
    There are many other ways to be inclusive and not alienate your audience members; however, these were some that novice speakers could grasp and immediately incorporate into the speeches assigned in the course; it is the author's hope that you will continue the study of public speaking and gain further knowledge of other strategies of inclusion.

Chapter 7

Nonverbal Communication

Learning Objectives

Exploration in this chapter will allow students to discover:

7.1 Defining and Understanding What Nonverbal Communication Is
7.2 The Body Speaks Loud and Clear/Nonverbal Mistakes/Actions Will Dominate Words
7.3 The Nonverbal Communication Categories
7.4 Reading Nonverbal Body Language/How to Improve Nonverbal Encoding

© Robert Kneschke/Shutterstock.com

You've bestowed upon me warmth with your smile, comfort with your embrace, and admiration with those eyes, in doing so you have spoken truth abundantly to my heart . . . no words needed.

— Authors own

Summer is over and the fall brings in a new semester at the community college where Dr. Katy Veal is department head of the Language and Communication School. Before each semester begins, she and every other faculty member are expected to attend a convocation, which includes a meeting on new policy and developments for the academic term. Following said meeting, lunch is served while various recognitions and awards are presented. After which all faculties must report to their respective departments for individual semester prep faculty meetings. Veal is a bit concerned about this term due to new changes set by the provost she has to implement while facilitating the meeting that will not be favorable to many who teach in the department.

Scenario

© Monkey Business Images/Shutterstock.com

Veal enters the room and observes four colleagues: Terry, Rachel, Gail, and Simon, sharing details of their summer vacations while waiting for the meeting to start. While the sign-in sheet is passed around to each faculty, she approached the lectern, took a deep breath and began.

"Good evening, I hope each one of you have enjoyed your summer break and are preparing for a great fall semester. I will be as brief as I can because I understand the hard work that goes into getting ready for a new term and new students. Several meetings still have to take place among each department after this one and you need ample time to do so. Also, I would like to have plenty of space for questions, so let's get started. The provost has set forth new guideline for us this term that have to be implemented immediately. First, the request for more faculty visibility on campus, the nine hours that each of you have for office hours must increase to an hour per course credit taught, not to exceed twelve hours."

Veal was not surprised at their reactions: she heard sighs and groans; Terry folded his arms, Rachel frowned while shaking her head while Simon and Gail gave each other a glance of disappointment.

"It has also been decided," Veal hesitated, before continuing, "that all adjunct faculties will now be on 4.5 month contracts instead of 9 months, which means that all faculties will not have contracts available until next month in September. Along with that, this semester we will now have mandatory faculty meetings every other Friday at 4:00 o clock."

Terry interrupted, "So let me get this right, our contracts are changing to four and a half months and we have to start the session without a signed contract, that's a blow to the head. Not to mention, the every other week faculty meetings; what about those of us on a Tuesday Thursday teaching schedule, and who commute from the city, it just doesn't seem fair to us at all."

Veal nodded, raised her hands and said, "I understand your concerns. The contract situation is a brand new development and as department heads we are all highly concerned about the impact this could have on departments as our adjunct faculty make up more than half of the faculty and are a vital part of the functionality of any institution of higher learning. You are not alone; we have questions about it too and will be meeting to address our concerns next week. To address the faculty meetings, we feel it necessary to connect more and monitor the various committees' progression in each department to be certain our individual goals are met and in compliance with campus policy. I'm going to ask that you all bear with us through this semester; it will be modified next term. This was the schedule I was given, so we all have to make some adjustments."

Simon briefly covered his face in exasperation; Rachel jotted something on her agenda and passed it to Gail, while Terry said, "It just appears that we are being asked to give a lot more than we are getting in return which does very little for morale." Several faculty nodded in agreement and others responded with the "uh ah" sound.

"Any questions or concerns?" Veal asked, looking at the clock on the back wall. No one responded, so she dismissed the faculty meeting. Simon abruptly left the room, Terry began to chat with Gail and several other faculties, and Rachel looked distraught as she gathered her things and quietly left and went to her office.

Veal stopped in Rachel's office to speak to her privately and noticed her at her desk with her head in her hand. She said, "Rachel I noticed how upset you were about the new changes."

Rachel looked puzzled. "No not exactly, that is one thing that is certain . . . "change" and we have to adapt." "I just noticed that look of frustration on your face while visibly shaking your head even passing a note to Gail, and you never made eye contact with me again."

Rachel sat up straight and looked directly at Veal. "You totally misunderstood. I wasn't trying to avoid looking at you. The note I wrote Gail was to express my concerns of the arrangements my sisters and I have for the care of our aging mother. My day has been every Friday for the past three years. I was trying to figure out a strategy and became distracted I'm afraid. Honestly, I am fine with the contract situation as these things usually work themselves out and the office hours will provide more time for students and grading."

"Well you certainly appeared to be upset to me," Veal insisted. "I can assure you, I am not. I can easily adapt to the other changes, but my sisters and I made mother's schedule according to each of our work schedules. I apologize if I came across as angry. I know you didn't make the rules and you are just the messenger. There is no reason for anyone to be angry towards you. Everyone will adjust to the policies soon; some people are just allergic to change."

Veal smiles pleasantly. "That's reassuring, because the tension I felt was a lot different. I just want everyone to know that I am working hard for the department and I have their best interest at heart."

Keep this opening scenario in mind, identify the nonverbal categories of communication that Veal observed and caused her confusion.

7.1 Defining Nonverbal Communication and Understanding Some Basic Properties

Nonverbal communication can be a bit complex, as in the opening scenario individuals are left with the task of deciding whether or not to trust another person's nonverbal reactions when it conflicts with their explanation. When we communicate we send more than just verbal messages—we also send multiple nonverbal messages. Many times nonverbal messages are perceived to have more effect than that of verbal messages. As we know, verbal communication has limitation, and in many areas of communication nonverbal is more effective and efficient, for instance, explaining the shape of something, giving quick directions, or communication when it is not possible to speak at the moment. For instance, to tell someone to be quiet, you would put your index finger up to your lips; if all is well you may give a thumbs up; to indicate your anger you would raise your fist; to express you were not feeling well you would hold your stomach; to flirt you would blow a kiss at a person (or pull their ponytail), an expression of love, a heart made with the hands, and the list could go on and on.

Also, nonverbal messages tend to be more genuine as they are not controlled as easily as spoken word. They can also state feelings that are inappropriate to state publically because our social etiquette limits what can be said but nonverbal cues can communicate those thoughts for you. The nonverbal channel is useful in sending complex messages; speakers are able to deliver powerful thought provoking and memorable messages when the incorporation of nonverbal communication exists.

Nonverbal Communication Defined

The term nonverbal communication was introduced in 1956 by psychiatrist Jurgen Ruesch and author Weldon Kees in the book *Nonverbal Communication: Notes on the Visual Perception of Human Relations*. Nonverbal communication has been defined as communication without words. It includes signals, signs, and apparent behaviors such as facial expressions, eyes, touching, and tone of voice, as well as less obvious messages such as dress, posture, and spatial distance between two or more people. In Chapter 6, we learned the concept that words do not have meaning, people have meaning. People assign meanings to words as well as nonverbal signs.

Nonverbal meanings are unique to individual cultures and are created by how people interact with one another within them. They are influenced by social and psychological aspects of their frame of reference as well as the meanings that derive from those behaviors. Consider the part of the definition that relates to signals and signs. Each of us is bound by the element that is communication. We do not have the will to not communicate; communication will occur in some form even when one's desire is not to communicate. Being it total silence or no eye contact, your signals are communicating to others that there is an issue.

Everything communicates, including material objects, physical space, and time systems. Although verbal output can be turned off, nonverbal cannot. Even silence speaks.

Our scenario holds in it nonverbal signs that were misread or misunderstood; this happens all too often when a person draws meaning from your behavior, the meaning comes more from their interpretation of your behavior than from what you might have intended to communicate. Which is a clear indicator that efforts must take place to become a better decoder of other people's nonverbal communication; we will develop this further in this chapter.

As you can see, nonverbal communication can be a bit complex, even tricky, on occasion. Does your nonverbal communication always say what you intend for it to? If not, then you must make it a priority to become a better encoder of messages that you send, so that they in fact convey your authentic thoughts and feelings.

Much of our interpretations of what has occurred in our communication transactions with other people have little or nothing to do with language. It is, however, in large part the result of all the nonverbal aspects of the transaction. What nonverbal interpretations do you think the two women are making of each other in the photo here? You are now informed of what nonverbal communication is, next we will learn about the basic properties of nonverbal communication.

© fizkes/Shutterstock.com

Properties of Nonverbal Communication

Nonverbal communication is developed at an early age. Children are more adept to reading nonverbal cues than adults because of their limited ability to speak and their reliance on the nonverbal to communicate. As children develop verbal skills, their nonverbal communication does not diminish, they become intertwined in the total communication process thus enhancing and strengthening their communication.

As stated in Chapter 6 language is governed by rules of grammar, punctuation, syntax, and composition, and is not limited to just spoken word but also includes written as well as oral modes of expression. But a nonverbal signal, no matter how widely recognized or understood like a wave hello, or a peace sign, is not part of a formal language, meaning there are no rules of grammar or punctuation. Moreover, while we need to learn a language, many nonverbal signals comprise a biologically shared innate form of communication that we generally do not need to learn. Here we briefly consider four basic properties of nonverbal communication (Remland, 2009).

1. **Universality**

   The first property is that many nonverbal signals are universal, used and recognized by all. For instance, crying means you are sad, smiling means you are happy, hugging expresses comfort, nodding means yes, and moving the head from left to right means no. Our uses and interpretations of these signals are based on the context in which they occur. There is some form of nonverbal communication everywhere.

2. **Spontaneity**

   Several nonverbal messages can occur at the same time; many signals are received and sent spontaneously. They happen automatically, outside of our conscious awareness for instance, when a driver (parent) has to stop abruptly it is automatic to extend the right hand to protect the passenger (child). When someone surprises you, it triggers a spontaneous expression on your face, (sending a signal), which triggers an automatic response in the person who sees our face (reception of signal). In both cases (sending the signal and receiving it) the brain response before the exchange registers in conscious thought, hence the biologically shared hardwired system of communication.

3. **Iconicity**

   The third property of nonverbal communication is that many nonverbal signals are iconic; they may actually resemble or graphically represent the thing they are referencing. For example, tattoos are iconic forms of expression (e.g., tattoo of a sailor's anchor or sexy pinup) as are iconic gestures and body language that mime some kind of action
   (e.g., reading a book). This property is unique to nonverbal forms of communication because the words in a language do not look like what they are (e.g., the word *house* does not look like a house).

4. **Simultaneity**

   The fourth and final property of nonverbal communication is that many nonverbal signals occur simultaneously, unlike speech being a single channel of communication that conveys messages one word at a time, nonverbal communication conveys messages through multiple channels at the same time. In contrast, nonverbal communication allows sender and receiver to assume different roles and send message at the same time as well.

7.2 The Body Speaks Loud and Clear

Exploring the basic properties of nonverbal communication will hopefully broaden your perspective on this important form of messaging, and will also aid in how you look at it concerning body language as we discuss in this section.

Public speaking is just that "speaking" but it is never fully effective without the accessories of nonverbal communication. Body language is a key skill in public speaking, and the author's desire is to assist you in the use of proper technique during your presentations assigned in this class and beyond with presence and power.

Readers may ask: how important is body language? The answer is "it's vital" if your goal is to have the ability to influence, captivate, and give a memorable message to an audience. "You" are your most essential visual aid, your voice too is physical therefore you should realize just how much how you look and sound matters.

Never think of public speaking without thinking "Body Activation" because it is the incorporation of your content and character that will work in unison in delivering an effective speech. Follow these steps to ensure speaking success, remember the body speaks loud and clear, your body language will tell your audience a great deal about you, so it is up to you to decide what they walk away thinking.

Self-Visual Aid

© Vladyslav Starozhylov/Shutterstock.com

© Maridav/Shutterstock.com

You are in fact the beginning of your presentation, the first picture in the slide show if you will. Your audience will assess your appearance and determine if they like you and want to hear what you have to say. Being that "self-visual aid" should not only be about preparing for the audience, it should first start with you, how do you want to feel, what do you want your clothes to say to you and others? Should they say "I'm powerful, in control, and confident?" When you dress in a certain way, it helps shift your internal self" (Baumgartner, 2012). In her book *You Are What You Wear: What Your Clothes Reveal About You*, Baumgartner explains what messages your clothes are sending and how you can use your wardrobe to change how others perceive you—and even how you think about yourself. So begin with the thought process that "I should look good to be understood."

I'm Closed and Insecure

© photodoc/Shutterstock.com

The image above speaks volumes; the nonverbal signal with the hands clasped says "I am closed," which indicates to an audience that you are not accessible to them. Head down indicates that a person is insecure.

I Am Open

© Hans Kim/Shutterstock.com

The extended hands tell the audience that you are open, accessible, and inviting. This will aid in the positive responses that you desire from your audience members.

Warmth

© Rawpixel/Shutterstock.com

When you give a nice smile to your audience it says that you are warm and relaxed, it also relaxes your audience and promotes positive energy as well. Keep smiling!

Mind Your Posture

Correct posture: standing straight, shoulders back, and head up says: I am engaged, ready, and confident. This also ensures that when your body is in this "power posture" you will be in the prefect position to maintain eye contact with your audience; they will perceive you as having authority of the topic, as professional, and will be eager to hear what you have to say.

© VGstockstudio/Shutterstock.com

Straighten Up! / No Slouching

We have heard this from our mother since we were kids, to stop slouching "sit up straight" or to "stand up straight" well . . . you should have listened to her. It is beneficial for good health; helping you to avoiding back, shoulder, and neck pain, not to mention what things slouching indicates about you to the world. Slouching says "I am bored, disinterested, defy authority. I am sad, depressed, and powerless." Again, be mindful of your posture, audience members can pick up on these nonverbal signals and respond accordingly . . . not in your favor.

© NFstudio/Shutterstock.com

Shifty Feet

When speaking to an audience it is wise to avoid the shifty-footed dance of the terrified orator. Rocking back and forth, swaying side to side and pacing even. This shifting of weight from one place to the other is seen as a negative cue, says that you are emotional, experiencing body discomfort and desire to leave; it's time to wrap things up. Your audience will experience feelings of being rushed, tossed content mindlessly, and know that they are not a priority. To rectify this behavior, use the V stance, standing with feet in the V position to gain control of your excessive movement and avoid distractions.

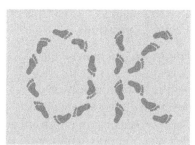

Indeed the body speaks loud and clear, so remember to be aware of the messages your body is sending out. Dress for the outcome you desire, be open and approachable to your listeners, smile to convey warmth, mind your posture to express confidence, no slouching, and remember to corral those feet.

© alexcoolok/Shutterstock.com

7.3 The Nonverbal Communication Categories

Extensive details have gone into nonverbal communication in this chapter; you may feel that you have a firm understanding of what it all encompasses. But wait, there's more: this form of communication must be carefully considered as there are vast components that make understanding a bit complex but if you are to be an effective and competent nonverbal communicator you need to understand the vocabulary. There are six main categories of nonverbal communication: kinesics, proxemics, haptics, chronemics, paralanguage, and artifacts. Each one of these categories includes various types of nonverbal communication.

Kinesics

Scholars refer to *kinesics* as the study of nonlinguistic bodily movements, such as gestures, facial expressions, eye contact, and movement as a systematic mode of communication. Kinesics is also known as the synonym for nonverbal communication called *body language*. Body language is significant to communications and relationships, and something modern society tends to miss out on when texting, emailing, or using Facebook and Twitter. The relevance of kinesics are high, many areas of society rely on it, i.e., law enforcement, counseling and psychology, medical and healing fields and any other professions where communication is physically observed. In our personal lives it is relevant in relationships of all kinds: parental, intimate, friends, work, or when making major purchases of any kind, like a home. Furthermore, it is extremely relevant when meeting someone for the first time. We will now briefly cover the element of kinesics.

Gestures

Gestures are movements of parts of the body, especially a hand or the head, to express an idea or meaning. Many of us know people or may be that person who seems to talk with their hands; most times we are unaware of just how often we all do it. Gestures are a way to convey meaning without using words; they are also used to emphasize our verbal messages. These frequently used gestures are often culture-specific. Let's use the "V" sign for example; this sign has two formats: one with the palm faced outwards, and another with the palm inwards. In the United States, both ways refer to "victory" and peace: protesters against the Vietnam War and activists adopted the gesture as a sign of peace. Because the hippies of the day often flashed this sign (palm out) while saying "Peace," it became popularly known (through association) as the peace sign.

© photkaShutterstock.com

In other places, such as in the United Kingdom, Australia, and South Africa, the same gesture with the back of the hand facing the other person is considered to be extremely insulting (Busuu, 2015).

Facial Expressions

One of the first types of kinesics is facial expression which is one or more motions or positions of the muscles beneath the skin of the face. This nonverbal category has undergone some of the most extensive research as it is extraordinarily unique in how it is used to communicate; you can manipulate the mouth to express several feelings, the mouth can smile, frown, purse into a kiss, smirk in disgust, your eyes can wink, widen, narrow and roll, your nostrils can flare, you can raise your one or both of your eyebrows and many of these and other muscle movements can be done simultaneously.

Eye Contact

Eye contact is the way we make visual contact with someone through our eyes. Eye contact is one of the nonverbal communications that is used when attempting to read a person in relationships, counseling, and interrogations. Listed are some explanations of how eye contact is assessed.

Direct eye contact: truthfulness (however, practiced liars often fake this signal).
Direct eye contact when listening: attentiveness, interest.
Widened eyes and raised eyebrows: shock, or an opening and welcoming expression.
Rubbing eye or eyes: disbelief, upset, or tiredness (if the signal is accompanied by a long pronounced blink, this tends to support the tiredness interpretation).
Upward roll of eyes: exasperation, frustration, wants situation to end.
Frequent blinking: excitement, pressure (normal human blink rate is considered to be between 6 and 20 times a minute, depending on the expert. Significantly more than this is a sign of excitement or pressure).

Infrequent blinking: boredom (if the eyes are not focused), or concentration (if accompanied with a strongly focused gaze). Infrequent blink rate can also be accompanied by signals of hostility or negativity, and is therefore not the most revealing of body language signals.

Quick eyebrow raise: greeting, recognition, acknowledgement.

(Ekman, Sorenson, Friesen, 1969)

When exploring these eye contact behaviors were you able to identify with any of them through your own behavior or someone that you know?

Posture

Another important type of kinesics cue is posture, which describes an overall body position, the way we hold ourselves or position our bodies, intentionally or unintentionally sitting or standing. As mentioned earlier in the section "Mind Your Posture," we know that posture speaks volumes about a person. From siting in an erect posture or slouching down in your chair, your personality, mood, and your confidence level is able to be depicted by others. It also provides clues as to how we feel about ourselves, how we feel about our own confidence (or lack of it), how much energy we have (or are lacking), how enthusiastic (or unenthusiastic) we feel, or whether we feel certain and relaxed (or anxious and tense) (Johnson, 2012). Intriguingly, we all almost always adopt the same postures in response to the same emotions.

If you were to observe an optimistic, confident, and enthusiastic person, you would notice that they were standing tall or sitting erect with their chest out and head up displaying a smile that reflects their positive feeling about themselves.

Body Movements

There is also the potential for your body to have communicative potential. For instance a person running quickly out of a building has quite a different meaning to an observer than one who is slowly strolling about. A person with poor posture, or who is always looking down, may be giving off a signal that they are tired, uninterested, or maybe even shy and insecure. Our discussion of kinesics should have made our understanding clearer that the many ways we use our bodies to communicate encompasses an important form of nonverbal communication, and yet there are many other ways that we communicate independent of and beyond language.

Proxemics

You know that discomfort you feel when someone violates your space in an elevator, stands too close in conversation, offends you with bad breathe, and crowd your space bubble in the grocery store line. Well, anthropologist Edward T. Hall understood those feelings all too well and did groundbreaking research to understand and diagram those awkward little moments that make up one's typical day in the 1960s. Hall coined the word *proxemics*, which is the study of space.

Spatial changes give a tone to a communication, accent it, and at times even override the spoken word. The flow and shift of distance between people as they interact with each other is part and parcel of the communication process (Hall, 1959).

Proxemics can be described as the "four distance zones." Below are the details of each one, detailing both the near and far phases. The first of the distance zones are:

- **Intimate Zone—Near Phase**: from 0 to 1.5′—reserved for lovers, comforting, protecting, close friends, and situations requiring confidentiality. However, research shows that many people have trouble with the intimate and personal zones and cannot endure closeness to others.

- **Intimate Zone—Far Phase**: from 6′ to 18′—head, thighs, and pelvis are not easily brought into contact, but hands can reach and grasp extremities, i.e., caress one's face, touching of a person's arm or hand.
- **Personal Zone—Near Phase**: from 1.5′ to 2.5′ —reserved for close friends or when you are affiliated with a particular group, i.e., social club, choir for example. The kinesthetic sense of closeness derives in part from the possibilities present in regard to what each participant can do to the other with their extremities. At this distance, one can hold or grasp the other person.
- **Personal Zone—Far Phase**: from 2.5′ to 4′—this distance is when you are keeping someone at "arm's length"; it extends from a point just outside of easy touching distance by one person to a point where two people can touch fingers if they extended their arms. At this distance a person cannot easily get their hands on someone else.
- **Social Zone—Close Phase**: from 4′ to 12′—perhaps you would observe this distance in the workplace or meetings, during a casual gathering, or impersonal business.
  It is safe to assume that in this spatial situation nobody touches or expects to touch another person unless a special circumstance occurs.
- **Social Zone—Far Phase**: from 7′ to 12′—this distance would be seen in impersonal business in the workplace, for example when meetings are in progress, the distance across tables or across desk, or the space between receptionist and the two o'clock appointment. Also, consider the cubicle in offices that serve to isolate and distance people from each other; this distance makes it possible for them to engage and work with one another while not being uncomfortable or appearing rude and unapproachable.
- **Public Zone—Close Phase**: from 12′ to 25′—during the transition from personal and social distance to public distance, many important sensory shifts occur that are well outside the circle of involvement, engagement, and physically touching others.
  There is a shift in the volume of one's voice at this distance; the voice is loud but not at full volume and a person is mindful of words, phrases, and grammar when attempting to communicate with someone.
- **Public Zone—Far Phase**: from 25′ or more—the distance is reserved for important public figures: presidents, popes, celebrities and the like. See Figure 7.1 example.

As each zone is introduced, we presented both the "close phase" and the "far phase" to indicate the significant differences between them. Hall's study of proxemic zones were specific to the North American culture, therefore it may not apply to people in many other cultures.

Haptics

Haptic is another one of the nonverbal categories; it is the study of touch. It is said to be our initial most basic form of communication and necessary to survive. This category is closely related to the study of proxemics; in both cases we deal with space and territories—touch is usually a direct result of allowing others into our intimate space. Touch is an important way to communicate with others; it gives you a sense of knowing, connecting, and sensing. Without the sense of touch you would experience isolation and helplessness. Touching is both meaningful and powerful; it speaks volumes positively and negatively.

Positive Effects of Touch

When expressing emotions of love or friendship nothing is more endearing than a hug or embrace, a gentle caress of the face, or a kiss on the lips. Touching is the physical way in which we express our emotions.

Figure 7.1 Hall's Proxemic Zones Only Close Phases are Shown.

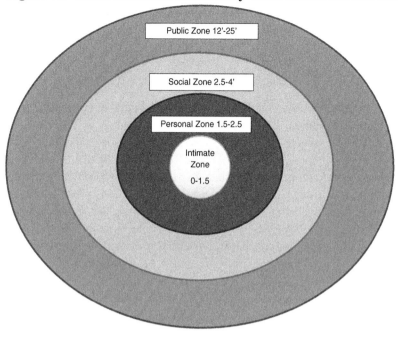

Genetically we all crave for the sensation of touch; from the time we were born it was that connection that created bonds with our mother. We are born with the desire to touch and be touched. Touch promotes

- Good health
- Intimacy
- Creating rapport and bonds with others
- Comfort
- Amplify meaning of verbal messages

Negative Effects of Touch

Touch can also be used to express one's aggression and anger through inappropriately striking someone to injure or gain control of them; this could be classified as domestic violence, random acts of violence, child abuse, or elderly abuse.

Touching could also be the culprit to unwanted contact; for instance in the workplace among co-workers, managers and subordinates, or college students, this would be classified as sexual harassment.

Types of Touching

- Pat on the back—act of comfort, showing sympathy, or pride
- Hug —greeting, intimacy, or comfort
- Handshake—greeting or leaving someone

- Holding hands—need for closeness, intimacy, or guidance
- Arm around the waist—protectiveness, intimacy, familiarity
- Pushing—anger, disgust

Chronemics

Do you have the time? Time waits on no man! Time is money! That's a waste of time!

You'll be late for your own funeral! Use your time wisely!

We have heard them all, but what do they really mean to you, how do you perceive time? We will explore the nonverbal category of chronemics, which is the study of the role of time in communications. This is a very important part of nonverbal communication, because through it we convey a lot about ourselves to others in the way we conceptualize time. Consider how your professor feels when students arrive late for class disrupting their lecture, the employee that is always late for their shift, or the parent who consistently arrives late to pick their student up from school. Moreover, consider what time means to you, and how you use it?

There are several conclusions that can be drawn about a person due to their use of time. The way we use time is most often dependent upon our perception of or relationship with another person. For example, if you are trying to make a good impression on the family of your significant others when you meet them for the first time, you are more careful to be punctual when arriving at their home for dinner than you may be after the relationship has been established for a more extended period. In a business meeting you are facilitating to secure financial backing for a new product you are launching in a reserved conference room at the Hilton Hotel, you would be mindful to be exceptionally early to prepare and troubleshoot any unforeseen issues that could arise before your potential investors arrive, to show professionalism and consideration for them in the hope of a successful outcome of negotiations. When a person books a flight it is understood that they will spend time waiting in long lines. They will also have to arrive at the airport several hours before departure to accommodate the time it takes for bag check-in and security checks by TWA officers; however, for travelers who may be late for whatever reason will suffer the fate of missed flights, rescheduled flight, or even the repurchase of flights. These examples illustrate the expectations about the use of time and how we attempt to modify it in relationships with others and situations.

The ability to understand time varies among people across cultures. You may have co-workers, family, or friends whose respect for punctuality may not mirror yours at all. Or perhaps you are the person with poor use of time. Culture in no way is the only factor that influences behavior; whatever the reason, it is important to monitor how your use of time is communicated to others. If you know that your constant tardiness is considered offensive and disrespectful to your partner, your professor, your child's daycare/school, your social club etc., it would be useful for you to consider what your motivations might be in persisting with that behavior. You should perhaps ask yourself if you are concerned about the impact your actions make on the people involved and do you care about how you make them feel? Many opportunities are lost; relationships of all kinds suffer, i.e., intimate, personal, and business, with abuse and misuse of time. Nevertheless, the good news is that unlike other types of nonverbal communication, the management of time can be easily controlled; however, it will take a diligent and conscious effort. Here are suggested tips to assist you in better time management:

- Create a daily plan
- Use a calendar
- Use an organizer
- Know your deadlines
- Know accurate details of events ahead; date, time, location, theme, rsvp etc.
- Target to arrive early not on time

- Have a clock visible and set at least 10 minutes ahead of schedule
- Prioritize
- Eliminate time wasters; Facebook, twitter, Instagram etc.

Time

How relentless is time passing as it does

Spending itself no matter our fuss

For it has a pace all its own

And to "save" it, well that notions gone

Every soul for it has need

More more is our constant plead

For there's only but 24 in a day

If given more would you waist it away?

For time is the essence of all our opportunity

Should we abuse its worth? What lunacy!

What precious gift to each it is bestowed

With too little gratitude ever shown

Our God allots each day its own supply

Fill it full; waste not, for it is sure to fly

8/23/07

— Author's own

Artifacts

Without debate the nonverbal communication category of *artifacts* is the most cautiously managed of all. Also known as artefactual communication, it is a social process in which individuals employ symbols to establish and interpret meaning in their environment (West & Turner, 2010). Research shows that there may be a correlation between how you dress and your identity (Powell & Gilbert, 2009). What would your home or office décor say to strangers about you? What would the car you drive, clothes you wear reveal about you to others who do not know you? What is your overall intent of communication when you choose what you will wear on a given day? Whether you know it or not you are sending information to others about yourself by displaying these artifacts.

Careful consideration is taken into shopping for one's clothing, shoes, jewelry, and handbags. Not to mention the effort that has been made to select the vehicle we drive or the house in which we will live. Humans are concerned with the image they project and the impression they make. Perhaps you want to be regarded as professional, successful or even affluent or powerful. Some may want to be perceived as trend-setters, having their own creative norms that express a unique trendy carefree style that will not live within the boundaries of societal expectations. Just be willing to live with the consequences of the message you send; if your choice of attire sends messages of disrespect for others or a disregard for the occasion, expect a response of disapproval.

Culture in fact influences artifacts in a great way. The way you dress, the furnishings in your home are in direct relation to the expectations and rules of your culture or co-culture group. Scholars agree that clothing has meaning and is a means of communicating socially acceptable confines of behavior in a certain place and within a certain period of time.

Expression of a sense of self and the identity of a culture is held in how people in a society dress themselves, whether it is wearing leather aprons or using yards of fabric in many layers to cover the whole body from view (Condra, 2013). Take in the beautiful elegance of the Indian traditional attire. The clothing traditions in India were formed by the influence of local climate, beliefs, cultural traditions, and different regional peculiarities. People of India wear ornate attires made from natural fabrics. They use a lot of jewelry and embellishment. Very often Indian garments consist of a simple large piece of cloth that can be draped in various ways. The national Indian female clothing is rather modest and feminine at the same time.

From Nigeria, the Yoruba prefer the beautiful bright outstanding garments of the gele; headdress for women, the elegant blouse known as a buba; also there is the traditional skirt, the iro. For special ceremonies like weddings the men adorn themselves in the traditional robe called the agbada worn over their clothes. What will your artifacts contribute to the conversation? They too have something to say.

Paralanguage

It's not what you say; it's how you say it. Nothing could be truer. The other five nonverbal components of a message are part of the impression of how something is said; but in situations where an actual verbal message is spoken, the "tone of voice" is quite significant. We are referring to paralanguage, which means vocal qualities such as volume and tempo that accompany spoken language are part of nonverbal communication. If a speaker changes even one of these aspects, the resulting meaning can be quite different to listeners. This is also referred to as vocalics, the study of how voice functions alongside language. Paralanguage encompasses a very wide range of vocal behaviors, all of which are intertwined to one or more or the four main attributes of the human voice: pitch, rate, volume, and vocal quality.

Pitch

Pitch is the degree of highness or lowness of a tone, created by the frequency of the sound waves produced by your vocal folds when they vibrate.

Rate

Rate is the speed of speaking in words per minute (WPM) from slow to fast, with normal rate averaging about 125–150 words per minute. Your rate, most times are determined by the emotion or the type of message you are communicating. For example; if you are excited about the new promotion you just received, you would be joyful and excited and thus would speak faster. News of a serious nature would be in a slower rate. However, effective speakers should always speak at a rate that his listeners can comprehend their message while also holding their attention.

Volume

Volume is the measure of the loudness or intensity or the softness of a speaker's voice. Volume is measured in "amplitude," the objective measurement of the degree of change (positive or negative) in atmospheric pressure (the compression and rarefaction of air molecules) caused by sound waves, meaning the intensity of force applied to the breath stream as it moves past the vocal folds. People who speak too loud may be perceived as aggressive and overbearing and are intolerable; speakers that speak too low and monotone could be perceived as shy, insecure, and without confidence. They either appear to have an unwillingness to communicate and will risk not being heard altogether many times.

Vocal Quality

A speaker has to consider more than content when speaking. We have covered pitch, rate, and volume but how do we manage those three when it actually comes down to delivery? Vocal quality is the manner in which you produce the sound of the voice, the fluency, articulation, and tone factor in immensely when considering vocal quality. Fluency is the flow of your words and can have a profound impact on whether your audience follows and understands you. A speaker cannot afford to continually make unintended pauses during a speech, it will irritate the audience and the speaker will appear forgetful and unfamiliar with the topic content, and risk losing the audience attention along with credibility. Make no mistake intended pauses are necessary and important in a speech. They are purposeful stops in a speech used to transition or used for dramatic affect and interest.

Articulation is also quite valuable in voice quality; it is of utmost importance that a speaker is able to fluently and coherently express their ideas and feeling to an audience. Also, the tone of a speaker's voice, which is the vocal sound in reference to its pitch, quality, and strength. Can you use a variation of tones to fit the content of your message? If you are illustrating excitement can your voice accommodate that mood, if you intend for your audience to feel a sense of compassion can your tone take them to that place? Skilled speakers are able to use their tone to navigate their listeners' thoughts and moods when speaking.

Fillers

Whatever you do please avoid the temptation to use verbal fillers. These are words, sounds, or phrases inserted into sentences that replace natural pauses and that fill in gaps in our speech as we think about what to say next. These fillers contribute nothing to the verbal meaning of the sentence and are considered part of nonverbal communication. The fillers are like, um, you know, see, ok, I mean, right, uh and, constant sniffing. Speakers need to have their verbal filler radar on at all times; nothing is more annoying to an audience, and in excess it chips away at one's intellectual ability. Cut it out!

7.4 Improving Nonverbal Encoding

We all want to be understood, we can ensure this more times than not with verbal communication; however, it is a totally different situation when it comes to nonverbal communication. Unfortunately, many misunderstandings among family, friends, and co-workers result from nonverbal communication. Other people's interpretation of our nonverbal behavior are most of the times wrong but they will assume they are correct and act accordingly. If you are lucky you will have relationships in which other people will take the time to check out their perception of what you mean by your behavior.

We will briefly cover a few ways to improve your nonverbal encoding.

* **Self-awareness**
  One thing we have control to do is be mindful of our self and actions. If you desire to be perceived positively and become a better encoder, be cautious of the manner in which you use nonverbal communication. If you are aware you will see how others are responding to your nonverbal actions, if they are unfavorable then make modifications. As stated above, if you have someone assertive enough to check their perception of your behavior, you have the advantage to know how you are being perceived and take action.
* **Monitor Incongruent Behaviors**
  Make sure your words match your nonverbal behavior; for instance, if you tell someone you are OK with something they have suggested, but your facial expression is blank and when you say "sure that's fine with me" your arms are folded, you are speaking with a smirk, and rolling your eyes.

Research has shown that when words fail to match up with nonverbal signals, people tend to ignore what has been said and focus instead on unspoken expressions of moods, thoughts, and emotions.

- **Concentrate on Your Tone**

   Your tone of voice can convey a wealth of information, ranging from enthusiasm to disinterest to anger. Start noticing how your tone of voice affects how others respond to you and try using tone of voice to emphasize ideas that you want to communicate.

- **Consider Context**

   When you are communicating with others, always consider the situation and the context in which the communication occurs. Some situations require more formal behaviors that might be interpreted very differently in any other setting.

   Consider whether or not nonverbal behaviors are appropriate for the context. If you are trying to improve your own nonverbal communication, concentrate on ways to make your signals match the level of formality necessitated by the situation.

   For example, the body language and nonverbal communication you utilize at work is probably very different from the sort of signals you would send on a casual Friday night out with friends. Strive to match your nonverbal signals to the situation to ensure that you are conveying the message you really want to send.

- **Consider Cultural Meaning**

   This principle is extremely important in improving your nonverbal encoding skills. Always be aware of the various cultural meanings behind nonverbal behaviors. We have covered earlier in the text the wide variations in nonverbal norms across cultures. However, many people wonder whose responsibility it is to adapt to others' cultural preferences. Indeed, "When in Rome, do as the Romans do," this suggests that when you are a visitor in another culture, you should work to conform to their practices. Be mindful that these adaptations will not come easily for many, as most of the people with whom you will interact will not be adequately informed about the subject of intercultural communication. Moreover, the culturally competent communicator is not the person who insists that others adapt to his or her cultural preferences.

PART 3

Interpersonal Communication and Small Group

Chapter 8

Interpersonal Relationships and Conflict

Learning Objectives

Exploration in this chapter will allow students to discover:

8.1 Identifying Interpersonal Relationships
8.2 Relationship Development and Deterioration
8.3 Relationships and Social Media
8.4 Relationships and Conflict

© CREATISTA/Shutterstock.com

Personalities, idiosyncrasies, shortcomings, and loose lips all make up the beauty of what we know as relationships.

— Authors own

Scenario

Marlon and Vanessa are siblings who met up at their childhood home to ride together to a friend's party. Marlon is a computer engineer and an army veteran and the eldest of the two, while Vanessa is a cash analyst in the oil and gas industry. Once they arrived they came inside to greet their mother and teen sister as well as make a beeline to raid the refrigerator for refreshments, all with their usual chipper fun-loving attitudes. The pair left and shortly thereafter the selfies were sent to mom's cell phone of goofy funny faces of them and their friends indicating that the evening was off to a good start. It appeared that everyone had plans for that brisk Saturday evening and mom's house was the parking lot for abandoned cars of the teens that piled up in the chosen drivers car for the night, (more than likely the car that had the most gas in it) and mom prepare for a quiet dinner out. There is a place for everyone and everyone is in their place.

© pathdoc/Shutterstock.comç

Dinner was pleasant; now the evening is wounding down for mom and she is heading home, the hour is late, which means the usual heavy traffic is not a factor. As she pulls in her driveway, she notices her daughter's car still parked in the driveway and assumes she and her brother are having a late night out, but this thought lasts but a few seconds; headlights shine from Marlon's car as he slowly pulls into the driveway behind her.

Once out of the cars the normal greetings take place between them and their mother but something is amiss. Although the siblings are known to have a close and strong relationship, it is noticeable that they are at odds with one another. Everyone enters the house through the garage, Vanessa takes a seat on the couch, and Marlon stands near the stairwell near the garage door.

Immediately the two began to revisit the discussion they were involved in earlier while mom looks on saying nothing. Important to realize, the siblings regularly indulge in passionate discussions on world-views and the like but this time was different from any other. They were discussing politics, government, and the eradication of racism in America, the situation became volatile, tempers flared, they were over-talking one another, and even became verbally injurious at times, calling one another's stance "stupid!" As they furiously point fingers, flail their arms, and assassinate one another's views, their mother is in utter disbelief at this unusual behavior between them and has had enough. She wondered what could have transpired during the course of the evening to provoke the usually loving siblings to seemingly raise an all-out war against each other. Under those circumstances she is now forced to neutralize the situation, she then rises from her seat, looks at each one and authoritatively demands that they be quiet, end the discussion, and go to their respective homes. It was explained to them that a discussion is one thing and is always allowed but the injurious comments among them is unacceptable and will not be tolerated. Perhaps, they will give it a few days, reach common ground and work out their differences, but right now, throwing in the towel and a cooling-off period is what is needed.

Interpersonal relationships are unique and can face various challenges, think about the opening scenario, how do you think the siblings should have handled their disagreements and what possible outcomes do you think were a result of their argument?

8.1 Identifying Interpersonal Relationships

Interpersonal relationships are close associations between individuals who share common interests and goals, and compatibility with each other. Relationships are the strongest element in which humans survive emotionally, mentally, and spiritually. People must gel well in order to form healthy lasting connections with one another. To better understand interpersonal relationships we are going to go over the various types in the following.

- **Friendship**
  An unconditional interpersonal relationship that individuals enter into on their own free will and choice, there are no formalities; however, the requirement is that people must genuinely enjoy each other's presence.

  Friendships can be between
  Woman and Man
  Man and Man
  Woman and Woman

  Friendship Essentials
  Transparency is the most essential factor for a stable friendship.
  Do not hide things from your friends. Be honest with them.
  Guide them whenever required. Never give them any wrong suggestions or advice.
  Feelings like ego, jealousy, hatred, anger do not exist in friendships.
  The entire relationship of friendship revolves around trust and give-and-take.
  No relationship can be one-sided and the same applies with friendships.
  Try to do as much as you can for your friends.
  "Thick as Thieves!?" Never ask a friend to do something illegal, or unethical.
  My friend is "Ride or Die!" This is not literal folks. "I'll Ride but I don't wanna Die!"
  Know the boundaries of your friendship (trust me, boundaries do exist in friendships).
  Friendships are not territorial; your friends are not "your property."
  There is no such thing as "someone else is taking my place." Friends have the capacity for more
    than one friend. Perhaps someone needs to mature a bit.
  Seldom visits make better friends; every friend should be allowed to walk in their own space and
    breathe in their own air from time to time.
  Want to keep your friends? DON'T BORROW MONEY and if you must PAY THEM BACK!

- **Love**
  An interpersonal relationship characterized by passion, intimacy, trust, and respect is
  called *love*.
  Individuals in a romantic relationship are deeply attached and attracted to each other and share
  a special bond.

  Romantic relationships can be between:
  Man and Woman
  Woman and Woman
  Man and Man
  Cat and Dog
  Dog and Dog
  Cat and Cat (you get the picture)

  Romantic relationship essentials:
  A sense of respect and mutual admiration is essential.
  Two partners must trust and honor each other in this relationship.

Partners must reciprocate each other's feelings, which enhance the probability to stay in the relationship for a longer period of time.

Each person's goal should be to gain understanding to minimize conflict.

Passion is key in maintaining that strong barely controllable emotion and attraction, you felt initially in your relationship.

Intimacy promotes the connection, closeness, and familiarity between partners.

Love relationships have several structures; if two people decide to take their relationship to the next level they may marry and create a "formalized relationship" they will then stay together in a life-long "grabbing life by the horns together" situation.

Two people may be in love but choose not to marry and may or may not live together. If they decide to live together without formalizing the relationship, this is considered a "live in" relationship AKA "shacking up."

If the love relationship is between couples that live a far distance from each other, this is considered a "long distance" relationship.

- **Platonic relationships**

A relationship between two individuals without any feelings or sexual desire for each other is called a *platonic relationship*.

In such a relationship, individuals are just friends and do not mix love with friendship.

Many times these relationships are formed organically however; sometimes rules and boundaries have to be established, for instance, two people meet, they have this instant connection, commonalities, and laughter; one may think "he's hot," the other may think "she's not," but would like to maintain a great friendship. So the gentleman may say, "you are so awesome and interesting, meeting nice people and forming meaningful friendships are not easy but I believe I've just got lucky, how about joining me and my friends for game night Saturday and bring your significant other if you'd like the more the merrier." This is a nice way to let the person know this is nothing more than a friendship and there is no romantic interest.

Platonic relationships might end in romantic relationship with both the partners developing mutual love and falling for each other.

- **Family relationships**

People related through blood or marriages form a family.

Family essentials

Mutual love and respect

Understanding of differences

Honor for patriarch and matriarch of the family

Honor family traditions

Show up in family reunions, anniversaries, and Christmas dinner

Pretend to like your aunt's potato salad

Be understanding when your job is to always bring napkins and plastic ware to the dinner (no one will ever forget those crunchy mustard greens).

Be nice to your crazy uncle in the leisure suit and white dress shoes.

Just start eating your green beans when everybody else's eyes are closed during the too long blessing of the food.

Pray for the sanity of the crazy sister or brother that every family has.

- **Professional relationships**

Individuals working together for the same organization are said to share a professional relationship and are called co-workers or colleagues. Colleagues may or may not like each other.

Professional relationship essentials:

Professionalism in the workplace

Mutual respect

Minimize water cooler gossip/rumors

Do not steal colleagues' lunch form break room fridge

Respect authority

Follow chain of command

Offer assistance to colleagues'

Be a team player

Offer to take lunch orders every now and then

Wear appropriate attire to work, Wear appropriate attire to work (Did I repeat that?)

Respect boundaries; if you do not have a scheduled meeting or certain rapport with a colleague; know when you have over stayed your welcome in a colleagues 'office.

Busy bodies are naughty naughties

8.2 Relationship Development

Interpersonal Communication

Now that we have discussed the five types of interpersonal relationships, let's see how relationships develop. When we look at movies and fairy tales of "love at first sight," it all seems so beautiful and heartfelt; however, it simply cannot allow for what truly takes place in real relationships. What about how annoying it is when you learn that your "knight in shining armor" leaves his stinky rolled up socks all over the house and snores like a grizzly bear in his sleep and his good looks will only return when he awakes, or the "apple of his eye" that has terrible flagellants? All things will first appeal to what we can see initially about a person; however, so many unpleasant things are an innate part of the characteristics of those pretty presentations. Development of relationships is not possible without verbal and nonverbal communication and being able to understand and relate while accurately encoding and decoding nonverbal signals. Most are not concerned with the communication aspect of relationships when "love is in the air," not until chaos arises do we realize that communication was the problem all along but he was "just so adorable."

We know what interpersonal relationships are, but it is also important to know what interpersonal communication is. *Interpersonal communication* is the process by which people exchange information, feelings, and meaning through verbal and nonverbal messages: it is face-to-face communication. Most communication scholars, when examining interpersonal communication usually focus on the *dyad*; this means that they are interested in what happens in one-on-one communication. Not to say that interpersonal communication does not take place among groups of three or more people because it does. Simply put, the most beneficial method of looking at the dynamic of interpersonal communication, even in larger groups, is to study the situation as a series of multiple dyads in interaction with each other. Also, technology has changed the traditional means by which we do things, including forming relationships; these studies are now including online dating as well. Smith & Duggan (2013) said that 11 percent of American adults—and 38 percent of those who are currently "single and looking for a partner"—have used online dating sites or mobile dating apps.

One in every 10 American adults has used an online dating site or a mobile dating app. We refer to these individuals as "online daters," and we define them in the following way:

- 11 percent of internet users (representing 9 percent of all adults) say that they have personally used an online dating site such as Match.com, eHarmony, or OK Cupid.
- 7 percent of cell phone apps users (representing 3 percent of all adults) say that they have used a dating app on their cell phone. Interpersonal relationship refers to a strong association between individuals sharing common interests and goals.

    A sense of trust, loyalty, and commitment is essential in a relationship. Individuals need to trust and respect their partners to avoid misunderstandings and conflicts, and understand that it takes time for a relationship to grow and have the ingredients for longevity.

Defining interpersonal communication should now prepare you for the steps in relationship development. According to distinguished scholar Mark L. Knapp, every relationship, be it a friendship or of an intimate nature, is likely to go through one of the following stages.

Stages of Relationship Development

First Stage—Initiating

Initiation stage is the beginning of the relation, a brief period of time when we are getting acquainted with one another. The time is spent attempting to make a good first impression, you are concerned with your personal appearance, mindful to say and do all the right things, even laugh at all their jokes. You will be monitoring your verbal and nonverbal communication remembering to say all the appropriate things, to smile, make eye contact, and be well dressed. It is during this time that determining if further communication is desired by both parties will also take place.

Experimentation Stage

If the parties show initial interest, they may next start exploring, (also known as the probing stage) looking for common interests by engaging in low-risk topics, or exploring common acquaintances they both may share. This stage is reserved for surface *sunlit zone self-disclosure* (top layer near the surface) i.e., where you're from, travels, family size, college attended, or favorite sports team etc. This is not the stage during which one reveals their deepest darkest secrets, emotions, or opinions. If you do reveal such things, this stage could also be the "I'm outta here" stage. So if you like the person, keep a lid on the scary stuff.

In business relationships, there will also be investigation into what each person brings to the table that will add value to the business of the other person.

Intensifying Stage

With enough in common, the people now start sharing more private information and checking for reciprocal sharing by the other person that signals their interest in deepening the relationship. It is safe to say that the relationship is now becoming interpersonal as communication moves toward greater depth and breadth. This stage is reserved for *twilight zone self-disclosure* (deeper, more intense) i.e., past relationships, religion, world views, values and beliefs etc. This is when parties are spending more time together, acquiring "our" favorite song, movie, or restaurant. Also, this stage may include gift-giving, creating new memories and declarations of affection. Advances may be made for further intimacy to test for the desire to take things further.

© Monkey Business Images/Shutterstock.com

In business, this may include negotiation and contracting activity that will lead up to value creation and exchange.

Integrating Stage

The *integrating stage*, "parties" are now "partners" and they definitely come together. The two people now start seeing each other more often as they integrate a number of parts of their lives. Your social circles are intertwined as secondary relationships are formed with people who matter to the other. Romantically, this may include sharing of space, sharing resources, intimacy, high levels of concerns for well-being, and sexual relations. This is when *midnight zone self-disclosure* (deepest darkest extremely intense) occurs, deep disclosure of shameful secrets, i.e., what really happened between you and your ex or best friend, how you lost your second job due to stealing realms of copy paper, or the fact that your court date was not for traffic court, it was for the DUI you received last year after the New Year's Eve party.

Another behavior is that couples modify their schedules to spend all time that is not spent at work or with family with each other. Even verbal behaviors occur during this stage as well. The pronouns *I, you*, and *yours* are replaced by *we, us*, and *ours*. It goes without saying that who you were as a person has literally changed; you have taken on interests that were unknown to you before and forsaken others that are not shared by your partner.

In business, this is where they start working together with each getting value from the arrangement, often directly financial or one that will lead to financial benefit.

Bonding Stage

Finally, the two people are fully integrated in the bonding stage. Here they make their formal public statement of commitment known and may formalize it, for example through marriage or a live-in situation. Other symbols of undeniable commitment may also include joint bank accounts, investments like the purchase of a home, business ventures and having children. Major decisions are all inclusive and are usually never made without consulting the other.

It is important to realize that once this formal public statement is made, it is more difficult to end the relationship, due to legal and sometimes religious sanctions. Do consider that marriages and commitment ceremonies are incentives for couples to work out their differences to achieve successful relationship outcomes; they also give partners a sense of security in that disagreements are less likely to permanently affect the relationship.

In business, this includes partnership and trusting relations that reduce transaction costs and add longer-term value.

Relationship Deterioration

Unfortunately not everyone "walks off into the sunset" but the proverbial phrase "the wall's came tumbling down" does apply to many. Because we all understand that relationships do have the propensity to fall apart and the intensity with which relationships begin to deteriorate depends on varying circumstances. Once a relationship has advanced to the integration or bonding stage, dissolving the relationship often begins with significant conflict and advances through several *stages of deterioration*, which include differentiating, circumscribing, stagnating, avoiding, and terminating.

Differentiating

The *differentiating stage* mirrors that of the integrating stage in that higher deeper levels of self-disclosure and expressions of immense feelings are involved. Whereas the feelings in the relationship in the integration stage were mostly positive, those in the differentiating stage are of a more negative nature. The couples are no longer centered on how their union formed due to their commonalities, but more on their individuality and how they are different. At first, and with the pressures of living, the closely bonded joint relationship starts to pull apart as the people have demands of different jobs, different friends, and different interests.

In this stage verbal messages, which are often injurious to and critical of each other, are used in an effort to point out differences: "Who does that?" "Clearly we don't see eye to eye!" "A blind man could see that," "How many times do I need to tell you that?" "Why would you do that?" etc. Nonverbal messages can range from hostile facial expressions, earbuds in the ear to avoid interaction or ignore, the "silent treatment" and the withholding of intimate touching. Also, the personal pronouns established in the integrating stage shift from *we* to *I* and *you*.

Undoubtedly, the differentiating stage is one that is unpleasant and frightening; after a couple of years, people are no longer floating on a cloud and start to see themselves and the other person as individuals rather than a tight couple. Many times feelings of abandonment emotionally and physically, as well as feeling of betrayal, occur, especially if one or the other has given up great portions of themselves to accommodate the needs of social connection in the integrating phase.

In business, other customers, suppliers, and work pressure start to reduce the chance to meet. Individuals may also be looking to advancing their career.

Circumscribing Stage

As the people grow further apart, the focus moves toward setting boundaries and limits. People are now adamant about having their own individual space, their own possessions, and their own friends and so on. Partners draw a subliminal circle around topics that are not "open for discussion." These touchy topics are "off limits" as they have proven to be the culprit of inciting discourse. The partner's seem to agree not to talk about "how you never defend me when your mother insults my cooking and housekeeping skills," "we won't discuss how my brother asked to spend one night and has been here for three months," and "we absolutely will not mention our mess of a relationship." Due to the broken lines of communication, open expression of feelings are stifled as well as the negotiation of one's needs, thus intimacy has decreased. This stage will suffer a great deal of masking; the conflict exists; however, it is in disguise, couples go through the motions and repairing the relationship in the circumscribing stage becomes increasingly difficult because of communication restraints.

In business, there may be issues of quality and whether what is being delivered is that which is really needed. Conflict may cause recourse to contract details.

Stagnating Stage

A stagnant relationship has reached the stage where separation is complete in many ways, yet the relationship persists, perhaps through apathy, convenience, or other lack of need to completely separate. This stage resembles the experimenting stage in that its communication is at the surface and superficial, reduced to small talk: "how was your day?" "What time is your flight?" "Is there rain in the forecast today?" Their nonverbal interactions are without any enthusiasm at all, and signs of ending the relationship are visible.

In families, couples may stay together for the children even though their relationship has reached rock bottom. If tensions continue, it can be a difficult question as to whether separation is best or worst for the children.

In business, a stagnant relationship can lead to one or both parties receiving significantly less value than they once got from the relationship.

Avoidance

While some choose to stay in a stagnation stage, some will make the choice to head toward the termination stage, having first lulled through the avoidance stage. This stage is usually brief although not always. At some point the people see each other less and less, often deliberately avoiding contact. If they live together, one may go out whilst the other is in. If they work together, they may move jobs or otherwise ignore each other. In avoiding one another, one of the first things to go is eye contact (which may have faded long ago anyway). Even when in the same room, they will try not to look at one another. Communication if reduced to texting, note writing, or emailing and if verbal communication is necessary, it is brief statements and equally brief responses.

Avoidance also happens in business, where people see sorting out of a troublesome relationship or supplier as not falling into an area of comfortability, and so focus first on the issues that affect their key performance indicators.

Terminating Stage

Finally the people pull apart and go their separate ways. If there is joint ownership of houses, joint custody of children and so on then this can be an acrimonious and difficult stage. Many times expressions of sadness

Figure 8.1 Stages of Relationship Development and Deterioration

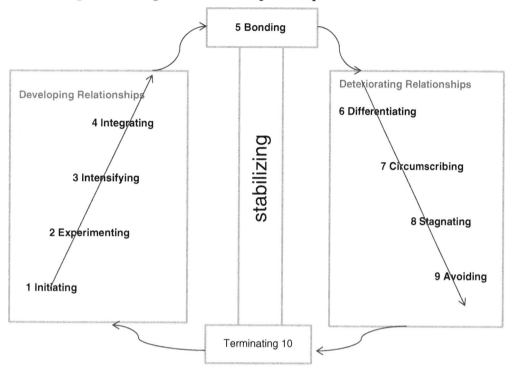

and remorse accompany the terminating stage and other times expressions of regret and hostility toward the partner as with situations of ending a relationship, it is not mutual for both people.

In business, this includes terminating suppliers, sacking employees and otherwise permanently breaking the relationship with the other person. See Figure 8.1 Example.

8.3 Relationships and Social Media

The author knows of a different time of dating when social media played no role whatsoever in matters of the heart. It wouldn't have mattered if you didn't "like" my picture or not, well . . . you better had because you'd have to come over to my house to see it. Even to this day the issue has never peered its ugly head; some things I prefer to remain the same and not comingle with technology. But that's the consensus of folk from a different era, who weren't born into the age of technology and had to adapt and conform. However, there are a set of norms in place in society, now when it comes to relationships that includes social media.

© Antonio GuillemShutterstock.com

Moreover, there have been problems of epic proportions because of it, for that reason this chapter will address common barriers to avoid using social media to increase the likelihood of better relationship outcomes. Relationships are all fun in the sun in the beginning, no one is seeing, or should I say they are refusing to see, anything questionable through their rose-colored glasses; for instance, the cell phone that's constantly morphed to the hand of your new love interest is overlooked, you ignore that they have not changed their status to "in a relationship" on social media, or that he is a chronic "Sir likes a lot" of every girl's sexy selfie.

Well in the beginning of your new relationship, you put forth a strong effort not showing insecurities, nagging, or having worries about the ex. Having a partner tell you in the beginning "I love that you are different from my ex who is insecure and nagged me all the time" is usually an effort to continue inappropriate behaviors without consequences. To combat this, set expectations early about respect, boundaries, and what is inappropriate behavior to you concerning social media.

Listed in the following are ways social media can affect a relationship.

Inappropriate Activity

A major red flag is when you see inappropriate activity happening on your partner's social media accounts. If he or she is liking pictures that make you feel uncomfortable, then it's time you speak up. If you are catching flirty comments or other questionable behaviors, it's your job to call it as you see it. That means if you catch your partner liking a person's Instagram picture of him/her wearing something sexy and it doesn't sit well with you, let him know. Or if your partner is adding random male/females on Facebook late at night, ask them about it. Be specific about what you saw and why it makes you feel unhappy. There may be an innocent explanation, but if it makes you feel uncomfortable, you have a right to speak up.

Too Private

It's OK to be private on your social media accounts. However, if your partner is too private, this is cause for suspicion. If he or she refuses to change their "Facebook Relationship" status from single or post any photos of you two together *anywhere*, then that is saying something bigger like "I'm not willing to abandon my past 'single life' behaviors, for you!" When you're excited about someone, you want to shout it from the mountaintops—or in our case, the internet. So it can be a warning sign when your significant other keeps your relationship hidden. If you want your partner to show more social media PDA (public display of affection), then simply communicate that to him or her.

Too Much PDA

On the contrary, too much PDA on social media sites can also be questionable. Thou doth post too much? Sometimes the couples that post too much are trying to overcompensate for their unhappiness and make it appear otherwise. (NOW HEAR THIS: EVERYONE KNOWS YOU ARE MASKING AND PERCEIVE THIS BEHAVIOUR AS PATHETIC.) It's always nice to leave a little privacy when it comes to a relationship. If you are in a relationship where you know it's not going well and you're arguing constantly, *and* your partner is still displaying too much social media PDA, then you might want to approach this topic and exert your over-posting energy into showing your partner that you are committed to actually working toward a real healthy relationship.

Attention-Seeking Behavior

If your partner is constantly posting selfies left and right, you might want to take a second look. Not at the photo, but at the relationship itself. It's OK to have a couple of photos of yourself here and there, but there is such a thing as one too many. If you feel as if your partner is posting photos of himself or herself to receive more attention, you are more than likely involved with someone that has a constant need for their ego to be stroked, and this is concerning and exhausting. Your other half should feel fulfilled within your relationship, instead of resorting to "likes" on his or her Instagram pictures for affirmation and a "CONFIDENCE BOOST."

Always On

Social media can become quite a problem if it's taking over your partner's life. If your date night is looking a lot like you talking and your significant other looking at his or her phone, you might want to shut it down, address the issue at once and if this behavior persists you don't want to be part of this.

Some people can become obsessed with this false sense of reality and lose sight of what is in front of their eyes.

Questionable Pictures

Pictures don't lie. Having said that, a questionable picture on social media that you don't like can say even more. If you are constantly seeing your partner in compromising pictures via the internet, it is time to pull their coat tale. You may not appreciate seeing your partner's ex holding her hair back while she bob's for apples at a Halloween party on Facebook. Or, seeing photos of your significant other "backing that thing up" or "dropping it like it's hot" with their ex on the dance floor in the dress you bought her would certainly alarm you. So if your eyes are unhappily burning, it's time to confront your questionable picture taker and express how you feel.

Facebook Snooper

Many have felt the need to play detective and snoop around your partner's social media accounts checking out their activity, probing into their past social media history sizing up the ex, looking at where they have traveled, their social interactions with friends, even when they posted "this is the love of my life" about the ex. Checking who liked your ex's pictures and causing yourself all kinds of anxiety. Well detective . . . when the "snooper" in you takes over there is a bigger issue at hand . . . INSECURITY!

Walk the Line

Snapchat, Instagram, and Facebook all give you the chance to walk a fine line between friendly, flirty, and downright shady. An innocent "hello" from an old friend can easily turn into that friend asking you to "catch up," then to inviting you to other things . . . it's important to know how to walk this line and to maintain appropriate boundaries.

8.4 Relationships and Conflict

There is conflict in all relationships. And by "conflict," we specifically mean verbal disagreements, silent treatments, and arguments. People disagree and that isn't necessarily a bad thing. In fact, you have the right to a different opinion from your partner. While conflict is normal, it can also be a sign that parts of your relationship aren't working. Human beings are complex creatures, and when you put two different personalities together, those complexities many times tip the scale. Consider the opening scenario when the two siblings Marlon and Vanessa were experiencing conflict in their relationship, although they are blood relatives their opinions are extremely different, raised in the same household, taught the same values and beliefs yet they clash. So one can only imagine the conflict possible with two people that do not share the same frame of reference. Although conflict in interpersonal relationships are inevitable, conflict resolution in relationships is possible as Ms. Carter has emphatically shown the world. Conflict resolution is a skill that must begin with understanding what conflict is and what causes it to spiral out of control, but what is certain, we must address it head on . . . Lemonade anyone?

© Featureflash Photo Agency/Shutterstock.com

Defining Conflict

"From a communications standpoint, *conflict* is an expressed struggle between at least two interdependent parties who perceive incompatible goals, scarce resources, and interference from the other party in achieving their goals" (Hocker, Wilmot, p. 23). Expressed struggle captures the notion that conflict does not exist unless all the people involved know that the disagreement exists even if the expressed struggle is not verbalized. The fury you feel toward your partner for embarrassing you when the two of you bumped into his ex at a restaurant and he said to her "I hope the food's good, we're here because somebody's not as good a cook as you," well, Mr. insensitive has no clue there is a conflict unless you express it to him. The internal conflict you are likely experiencing is being dealt with intra-personally as you process and sort out your feelings of discomfort, but it is a constant source of your unhappiness until your partner is also aware of the conflict.

Distinction between Productive and Destructive Conflict

Productive Conflict

Productive conflict is an open exchange of conflicting or differing ideas in which parties feel equally heard, respected, and unafraid to voice dissenting opinions for the purpose of reaching a mutually comfortable resolution. Characteristics of productive conflict are:

- Individuals are not afraid to share conflicting opinions or ideas
- It is a creative process that reveals fresh insight and new possibilities
- It promotes a sense of acceptance and inclusion
- Commitment to the relationship is not withheld
- Relational growth is achieved when individual growth is celebrated
- Parties have mutual respect for one another
- The probability of longevity in relationships are higher

The stronger your ability to engage in productive conflict, the more reward and growth in the relationship. Conflict is inevitable, as parties have differing frames of reference, education, style, and ideas; simply having the wherewithal to understand that basic concept will allow for more meaningful resolutions to conflict. Why do you think companies hire different "experts" within an organization who possess different conflict resolution skills, life experiences, and education? Productivity will suffer with everyone sharing the exact same background and expertise; it just mirrors what is already there, leaving no room for varying perspectives, growth, and mobility. This is needed in every company as well as relationships; we also experience relational growth and more fulfilling outcomes as a result of these various characteristics.

Destructive Conflict

Destructive conflict often flows from narrowly defined or rigid goals, and most often produces negative results. Individuals involved become less flexible and assume that the opposing party must suffer defeat. Involved parties succumb to personal attacks, threats, and a general tone of hostility. It goes without saying that this type of conflict is counterproductive and can become both emotionally and mentally devastating. Characteristics of destructive conflict are as follows:

- Both parties are unhappy with the outcomes
- Parties feel that they have lost
- Conflicts often escalate

- Conflict usually destroy the relationship
- Ignores real issues between conflicting parties
- Power struggle is usually the blame for destructive conflicts
- Destructive conflict originates primarily from feelings of inadequacy and hopelessness
- Parties have a fear of change and personal vulnerability
- Lack of empathy, inability to understand the views of others (Meehan, 2015).

Destructive conflict leaves relationships, whether intimate, friends, family, or work, with feelings of inequality and an imbalance of power thus damaging and most of the times ending the relationship altogether. When people feel judged negatively they lose confidence and begin to self-doubt; they will also become frustrated and resentful, prompting the desire the get even as opposed to dealing with underlying issues.

Conflict Styles

Just hearing the word conflict makes one think of a problematic situation, it is certainly thought that conflict should be avoided at all cost. Not necessarily so; conflict can come from a variety of sources, it can be a source of growth and transformation or a result of conflicting goals and priorities or a lack of shared goals between parties. Often we find that there are personality conflicts, when there is no chemistry with someone and you find difficulty figuring out how to click with the other person. We all have our own style of dealing with conflict and our style may conflict with another's which in turn may cause conflict as well but adapting to conflict style can be achieved. Finally, we will discover how we can also find conflict in values. Now our values are core, adapting to styles is one thing but adapting to someone's conflicting values is something totally different. Let's look at the five conflict styles and see if you can see which style you can relate to when dealing with problems and potential conflicts.

The Passive Style

The *passive style* is adopted by people who are uncomfortable with open conflict. They deem their needs as unimportant but the other party's as important. Passive communicators have the following behaviors:

- Denial. "What conflict? We are perfectly fine."
- Avoidance. "No worries, we never have to discuss that again."
- Accommodation. "Whatever you like is fine with me."

The Passive-Aggressive Style

The *passive-aggressive* style is when people appear passive on the surface, but are actually acting out their anger in indirect or behind-the-scenes ways. Passive aggressive communicators have the following behaviors:
- The silent treatment.
- The innocent approach. "I was only trying to be helpful; I didn't mean to offend anyone."
- The joking approach. Insult or cruel joke at partner's expense and then hassle them for lack of humor when they appear injured by your behavior.

The Aggressive Style

The *aggressive style* is about winning—often at someone else's expense. An aggressive person behaves as if their needs are the most important, as though they have more rights, and have more to contribute than other people. It is an ineffective communication style as the content of the message may get lost because people are too busy reacting to the way it's delivered. The Aggressive Style have the following behaviors:

- Habitual explosive anger
- Exaggerated verbal and nonverbal expressions
- Demanding and abrasive
- Frightening, threatening, loud, hostile
- Out to win, be seen, be heard, and intimidating to more passive styles
- Avoids conflict with assertive style as they are unable to intimidate
- Prey on more passive styles
- Intimidating
- Is a Bully

The Assertive Style

Assertive communication is born of high self-esteem. It is the healthiest and most effective style of communication—the sweet spot between being too aggressive and too passive. When we are assertive, we have the confidence to communicate without resorting to games or manipulation. We know our limits and don't allow ourselves to be pushed beyond them just because someone else wants or needs something from us. Surprisingly, however, Assertive is the style most people use least. Assertive styles are as follows:

- Socially and emotionally expressive
- Achieve goals without offending others
- Protective of own rights and respectful of others' rights
- Makes choices and takes responsibility for them
- Asking directly for needs to be met, while accepting the possibility of rejection
- Accept compliments and is liberal at giving them also

Submissive Style

This style is about pleasing other people and avoiding conflict. A submissive person behaves as if other peoples' needs are more important, and other people have more rights and more to contribute. Submissive behaviors are:

- Apologetic (feel as if you are imposing when you ask for what you want)
- Avoiding any confrontation
- Finding difficulty in taking responsibility or decisions
- Yielding to someone else's preferences (and discounting own rights and needs)
- Opting out
- Feeling like a victim
- Blaming others for events
- Refusing compliments
- Inexpressive (of feelings and desires)

Chapter 9

Small Group Communication

Learning Objectives

Exploration in this chapter will allow students to discover:
9.1 The Characteristics of Successful Small Groups
9.2 The Difference between Groups and Teams and the Three Types of Groups Used Most
9.3 The Steps of Group Problem-Solving Process
9.4 How to Be Effective Group Members and Group Leaders
9.5 Benefits of Small Groups for Students and Instructors and Group Speech Rubric

© Konstantin Chagin/Shutterstock.com

*Creative genius, inspiration, and brilliance beyond measure are often cultivated
in a small group . . . where will your next idea flourish?*

— Authors own

Sydney had rushed from her dorm to get to the student center to meet her group members. She set her alarm so she would not be late and they would get started on time. She was responsible for scheduling group meetings and was mindful to confirm meeting times with the other four members earlier. Her communication professor stressed the importance of starting and ending the meetings on time as everyone has really busy schedules and plenty of other things to do. Also, she had read the instructions for the project the professor had given in class but was unclear on some of the details; she was hoping to get help from the other members when they arrived.

Scenario

©goodluz/Shutterstock.com

Amber arrived after Sydney. Sydney and Amber never really spoke to each other much in class but she seemed nice and smart as she always participated in class discussions. "Hey there," Amber greeted her. "Are we the only one's here?" "It appears to be that way. I really hope this is not going to be the normal behavior for this group, we only have an hour to meet and I would hate to have to waist it waiting on people to arrive which will result in an unproductive meeting."

"My concern is that those of us that show up put everything together, assign roles, do the research and the people who do not participate during the process will show up near the end demanding changes and input that is too little too late so as to appear to have done work; that's really frustrating," Amber explained.

"I really dread group work for that same reason too. But that is why Professor West expressed in class that the project is not a 'one grade fits all' if you did not participate as required a peer evaluation would be assigned for this project explaining each members work habits and he would record those grades accordingly. That should be motivation for members to step up, but it is thirty minutes past the hour as we speak," Sydney added.

"You would think it would be motivation" Amber said. Not everyone is as focused when it comes to group work and how it affects everyone else involved. I see Kayla coming in now wander what her excuse is for being so late."

Kayla entered the room seconds later. "Hey guys sorry I'm so late, me and my boyfriend were at the movies, what did I miss and where is everybody else?"

Sydney and Amber looked at each other in disbelief; "We wish we had the answer to that question" Amber relented. "Well now there is three of us let's get this meeting started, the other two will have to be given what parts are left to do, besides I have an anatomy test to study for" exclaimed Sydney.

How have your experiences been working with groups? As we explore this chapter, see if you can see how some of the knowledge learned could have promoted a better outcome.

9.1 The Characteristics of Successful Small Groups

Defining Small Group Communication

Think about the opening scenario, does the activity in that group sound familiar—people not being on time, varying work ethics, and lack of motivation? It is common for individuals to dread group work yet it is a necessary part to life. Notwithstanding, most of what is accomplished in the workplace, education, and civic life are a result of decision-making by groups of various sizes. We will share valuable information in this chapter to increase your level of comfort in working in groups, which will aid in your success in the workplace as well as your educational endeavors. Both require the skill set of small group dynamics and the ability to work in teams.

Small group communication is a small number of people who have multiple face-to-face meetings over an extended period of time and who interact to achieve common goals. Technology plays a role in the way groups function now with mobile apps such as GroupMe, which is like a private chat room for your small group, with free messaging that enabling members to coordinate project details, scheduling, and so forth. However useful, it should not replace actual face-to-face meetings as it cannot compensate for the benefit of verbal and nonverbal communication.

Characteristics of Small Groups

Size Matters

Usually the first question is what size constitutes a small group or team? Research shows that the optimum group size of five to seven is the most productive size, this provides for maximum participation (Kemeda et al., 1992). Five is large enough to provide inclusion of opinions, but not too large where it inhibits full participation by each member. Important too avoid, is having groups to large where some find it impossible to give input where others find it easier to take a less active role.

Communication

Daily communication in small groups during the project process is essential, it is the foundation of any group. This helps with changes, challenges, and overall productivity. This ensures that each member's efforts and input is considered. This can be done via group text messages or email. This also allows for group leaders to gauge member participation.

Commitment

Commitment is key in effective small groups. This means a commitment to your stated goals, commitment to attend, as well as a commitment to keep up with any project requirements. If communication is the foundation of small groups, commitment is the glue. Many groups will have those members who are there in name only and will jump on the wagon when deadlines are approaching or the date a project is due to receive unmerited recognition, reward, or grades. Understand that this is a testament of one's character; it speaks of your integrity and respect for others and yourself for that matter, there is nothing worse than being on "your" journey and using someone else's water canteen and food supply when you've exhausted theirs you will move on to some other unassuming sole. At what point will you run on your own stem, provide for yourself and not be a burden for others? Some day you will be forced to and the revelation of who you really are will be most shameful . . . can you live with that? Let's hope not.

Decision-Making Methods

Another characteristic of successful groups or teams are the decision-making methods they use. There are many methods and procedures used by groups and each is designed to improve the decision-making process in some way. Listed below are some of the most common:

- **Brainstorming**
  Brainstorming involves group members verbally suggesting ideas or alternative courses of action. The "brainstorming session" is usually relatively unstructured. The situation at hand is described in as much detail as necessary so that group members have a complete understanding of the issue or problem. The group leader or facilitator then solicits ideas from all members of the group. Usually,

the group leader or facilitator will record the ideas presented on a flip chart or marker board. Once the ideas of the group members have been exhausted, the group members then begin the process of evaluating the utility of the different suggestions presented. Brainstorming is a useful means for generating alternatives but does not offer much in the way of process for the evaluation of alternatives or the selection of a proposed course of action.

- **Dialectical Inquiry**

    Dialectical inquiry is a group decision-making technique that focuses on ensuring full consideration of alternatives. Essentially, it involves dividing the group into opposing sides, which debate the advantages and disadvantages of proposed solutions or decisions. A similar group decision-making method, "devil's advocacy," which requires that one member of the group highlights the potential problems with a proposed decision. Both of these techniques are designed to try and make sure that the group considers all possible ramifications of its decision (Barnett, 2015).

- **Decision by Vote**

    Notice that when referring to group sizes they are always odd numbers (3, 5, or 7); this prevents the possibility of a tie vote. This is a valid reason for making a group an odd number, but it assumes that all members will be present to vote (and they aren't) and that the group has determined decision-making should be done by a majority vote (not always true). This method can prove problematic in that it creates winners and losers and the people on the wrong side of the vote are dissatisfied with the results. This method should only be used for minor issues, like where meetings should be held, time of meeting, or if lunch should be provided for said meetings.

- **Compromise**

    This method is usually better than voting because here no one completely loses or wins. Every member has to give up something in order to reach the compromise.

- **Decision by Consensus**

    This is considered the preferred method of decision-making, by consensus or general agreement. Groups using consensus is committed to finding solutions that everyone actively supports, or at least can live with, instead of simply voting for an alternative and having the majority in the group getting their way.

Group Inclusion

Diversity research in the past was dominated by a focus on the "problems" associated with diversity, such as discrimination, bias, affirmative action, and tokenism (Shore et al., 2009). We define inclusion as the degree to which an employee perceives that he or she is an esteemed member of the work group through experiencing treatment that satisfies his or her needs for belongingness and uniqueness. Brewer argued that individuals seek to balance these two needs through an optimal level of inclusion in groups to which they belong (Brewer, 1991). Effective groups are inclusion-driven, in that they pride themselves on knowing how to appeal to each member's specialized contributions to the group. In doing so this fosters a sense of comradery, moral, and motivation, which results in a higher rate of participation, productivity, and positive group outcomes.

Group Diversity

Group diversity promotes a variety of perspectives, similarity in values, and commonality of goals. Diversity brings an array of frame of references and cultures thus multiple perspectives on conflict resolution and problem-solving solutions.

Absence of Groupthink

The practice of thinking or making decisions as a group discourages creativity or individual responsibility, members refrain from expressing their view for fear of being judged, criticized, or disbanded from the group. Groupthink is usually influenced by dominant leaders or an aggressive group member. If you have ever been on the opposing view of a group and felt that you would be labeled "not a team player" if you expressed those views so you decided to go along with the majority, you were then in the pits of groupthink.

Rules and Norms

The final characteristics of small groups deal with the way a group is structured. All successful groups have a certain code of conduct, called rules and norms.

Group rules are *explicit* codes of conduct that are unique to that group and are clearly spelled out both orally and in writing. Rules may include requirements for membership, fees, mission statements, by-laws, locations, attendance policies, dress codes etc.

Group norms, however, are *implicit* codes of conduct. They are not spelled out but are merely formed over time. For instance, a member brings in their nonmember spouse to a meeting and nothing is said, then someone else does it and it is continually overlooked, then nonmember attendance is perceived as the norm.

9.2 The Difference between Groups and Teams

While all teams are groups of individuals, not all groups are teams.

Groups are formed when these five distinguishing features are present:

- *Number of people will be small enough for all to actively participate.* This is why most seminar facilitators assign break-out groups during session so that each person has an opportunity to share their insight and opinions.
- *Interacting together to achieve common goals.* In a class project you all share the same interest of making a passing grade, even though your actual reason for taking the course may be altogether different, one may be taking it to boost their GPA to get into graduate school and the other to complete degree plan requirement.
- *People interact face-to-face.* This benefit to this is that members get to know one another's different qualities, cultural backgrounds, and establish a common frame of reference through shared experiences even building trust. Moreover, without face-to-face it is difficult to understand a nonverbal communication and instant feedback.
- *Members are selected due to similar characteristics or commonalities.* Most members of groups are a part of said group because the commonalities are shared. For example; in your class room the commonality is that each of you are students, enrolled in the same class, responsible for same assignments, and needing to complete course successfully.
- *Meetings over an extended period of time.* Members should meet to establish a sense of belonging, history, and identity. Also, regular meetings enable members to effectively solve problems within the group.

Teams

Although teams and groups are many times thought to be one and the same, however, there are some characteristics that make them slightly different and they are as follows:

- *Task oriented.* Teams require coordination of tasks and activities to achieve a shared goal.
- *Degree of interdependence.* Team members are interdependent since they bring a set of resources to produce a common outcome.

- *Degree of formal structure.* Team members' individual roles and duties are specified and their ways of working together are defined.
- *Familiarity among members.* Team members are aware of the set of people they collaborate with, since they interact to complete tasks and activities. Members of a group may have personal relationships or they may have little knowledge of each other and no interactions whatsoever (Boundless, 2016).

Types of Groups

There are many variations of groups, including support groups, training, social groups, and therapeutic groups. However, there are common distinctions when it comes to organizations, classrooms, and work environments, and they are as follows:

- **Task-oriented groups**—formed to solve a problem, creating a product or providing a service. In such groups, like a committee or study group, interactions and decisions are primarily evaluated based on the quality of the final product or output. The three main types of tasks are production, discussion, and problem-solving tasks (Ellis, Fisher, 1994).
- **Relational-oriented groups**—formed to promote interpersonal connections and are more focused on quality interactions that contribute to the well-being of group members. Decision-making is directed at strengthening or repairing relationships rather than completing discrete tasks or debating specific ideas or courses of action.
- **Cooperative learning groups**—this is a form of active learning where students work together to perform specific tasks in a small group. The end goal can only be reached when every member of the group contributes effectively.

9.3 Group Problem-Solving Process

There are several variations of similar problem-solving models based on American scholar John Dewey's reflective thinking process. As you read through the steps in the process, think about how you can apply what is learned regarding the general and specific elements of problems. Some of the steps presented in Figure 9.1 are straightforward, and they are things we would logically do when faced with a problem.

Figure 9.1 Basic Steps in the Problem-Solving Process

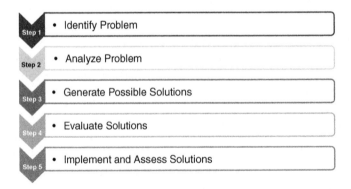

Problem-Solving Process, Step 1. Identify the Problem

Define the problem by considering the three elements shared by every problem: the current undesirable situation, the goal or more desirable situation, and obstacles in the way (McGraw-Hill, 2009, p. 229). At this stage, group members share what they know about the current situation, without proposing solutions or evaluating the information.

This step addresses the "what" of the problem.

Problem-Solving Process, Step 2. Analyze Problem

During this step a group should analyze the problem and the group's relationship to the problem. At this stage, group members can discuss the potential causes of the difficulty. Group members may also want to begin setting out an agenda or timeline for the group's problem-solving process, looking forward to the other steps. This step addresses the "why" of the problem.

Problem-Solving Process, Step 3. Generate Possible Solution

During this step, group members generate possible solutions to the problem. Again, solutions should not be evaluated at this point, but only be proposed and clarified. The question should be what could we do to address this problem, not what should we do to solve it. It is perfectly OK for a group member to question another person's idea by asking something like "What do you mean?" or "Could you explain your reasoning more?" Discussions at this stage may reveal a need to return to previous steps to better define or more fully analyze a problem. Since many problems are multifaceted, it is necessary for group members to generate solutions for each part of the problem separately, making sure to have multiple solutions for each part. Stopping the solution-generating process prematurely can lead to groupthink.

Problem-Solution Process, Step 4. Evaluate Solutions

During this step, solutions can be critically evaluated based on their credibility, completeness, and worth. Once the potential solutions have been narrowed based on more obvious differences in relevance and/or merit, the group should analyze each solution based on its potential effects—especially negative effects. Groups that are required to report the rationale for their decision or whose decisions may be subject to public scrutiny would be wise to make a set list of criteria for evaluating each solution.

Problem-Solution Process, Step 5. Implement and Assess Solutions

Implementing the solution requires some advanced planning, and it should not be rushed unless the group is operating under strict time restraints or delay may lead to some kind of harm. Before implementation, groups should also determine how and when they would assess the effectiveness of the solution by asking, "How will we know if the solution is working or not?" Certain elements of the solution may need to be delegated out to various people inside and outside the group. Group members may also be assigned to implement a particular part of the solution based on their role in the decision-making or because it connects to their area of expertise.

9.4 How to Be Effective Group Members and Leaders

Working in groups can be rewarding, but at times it can be difficult and downright frustrating. If there are poor communicators in your group, you may often feel left in the dark, confused or misunderstood. We will briefly discuss pointers on how to be effective group members and leaders.

Openness

Group members are willing to get to know one another, particularly those with different interests and back-grounds. They are open to new ideas, diverse viewpoints, and the variety of individuals present within the group. They listen to others and elicit their ideas. They know how to balance the need for cohesion within a group with the need for individual expression.

Prepare and Participate

This is an important characteristic of effective group members, they always prepare in advance before meetings. They have documents needed, talking points, any research needed, and well-written question and concerns. Equally important, they are willing participants in group discussions, assisting other group members if needed, and working with the group leader to fulfill group task roles to help meetings run effectively.

Use Problem-Solving Steps Effectively

We covered the problem-solving steps in the earlier section; now that we are addressing being an effective group member it is important that each member uses the problem-solving steps effectively to ensure group success. More than to be effective in your groups, problem-solving skills are highly sought after qualities in corporate America. Effective group members will understand the order in which problem-solving steps occur and know their importance. These are indeed people you want as a part of your group otherwise conflict has the possibility to become long drawn out ordeals, or groupthink will be the end result.

Listen Actively

Look at the person who's speaking to you, nod, ask probing questions and acknowledge what's said by paraphrasing points that have been made. If you're unclear about something that's been said, ask for more information to clear up any confusion before moving on. Effective communication is a vital part of any group, so the value of good listening skills shouldn't be underestimated.

Handle Conflict Effectively

Successful groups will be subject to some form of conflict during discussions, but how and who handles it makes a big difference. It should be handled with professionalism and by the assertive style, avoiding the passive, aggressive, or passive-aggressive style at all cost. The assertive style will be mindful to address conflict with all members having the opportunity to express their feelings and opinions with the freedom to be open and honest. The goal is to reach a win-win resolution to conflict that is agreeable to all parties.

Effective Group Leaders

As with most popular sayings, there is some truth in the adage, "Great leaders are born, not made." To some extent, the capacity for great leadership is innate. However, learning how to be a more effective leader is within everyone's grasp—whether you lead multiple teams, an entire company, or just five group members. Listed below are some valuable insights into being an effective group leader.

Effective Use of Power

Power is possession of control, possession of authority, or exerting influence over others. The five bases of power were identified by John French and Bertram Raven in the early 1960s through a study they had conducted on power in leadership roles. The five bases of power are divided into two categories as follows.

Formal Power

- **Coercive power**—power is gotten through threatening and punishing.
- **Reward power**—achieved by rewarding others for being in compliance with your wishes.
- **Legitimate power**—comes from having a position of power in an organization.

Personal Power

- Expert power—comes from your experience, skills, and knowledge.
- Referent power—comes from being trusted and respected.

As you can see, you don't have to be in a leadership or senior level role in an organization to have some form of power. However, effective leaders will use their power in a respectful manner that leaves each group member with their dignity.

Self-assessment

An effective leader will periodically take stock of their own personal strengths and shortcomings. They ask: "What do I like to do? What am I really good at?" "What are my areas of weakness, and what do I dislike doing?"

Responsive to the Group's Needs

Being perceptive can also help a leader be more effective in knowing the needs of the group. Some groups' value trust over creativity; others prefer a clear communicator to a great organizer. Building a strong group is easier when you know the values and goals of each individual, as well as what they need from you as their leader.

Leadership Traits

For someone to emerge as a successful leader, he or she has to have particular leadership traits, which makes the assumption that leaders are born—meaning that some people merely possess the traits that cause people to look up to them for leadership. They seem to be able to influence people with no real effort at all. There have been extensive studies associated with leadership conducted since the early 1900s, which reveal that such traits are intelligence, physical attractiveness, confidence, charisma, verbal skills, and many others. In more recent studies, Kellett et al. (2006) found that successful leaders seem to have more of these:
    Inspiration–Ambition–Creativity–Adaptability–Desire to lead–Confidence–Supportiveness, etc.

Leadership Styles

Consider the *leadership style* perspectives when viewing your leadership skills. This is also known as The Three-Dimensional theory of leadership:

- The Authoritarian *leader*—one who essentially makes the decision and imposes them upon the group.
- The democratic *leader*—participates with the group in deliberating and decision-making; the leader empowers the group members to actively participate.
- The *laissez-faire leader*—turns the whole process over to the group with little or no further involvement. Works well when members are trained professionals. See Figure 9.2 Example

Figure 9.2 The Three-Dimensional Theory of Leadership

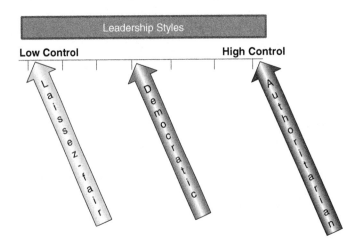

9.5 Benefits of Small Group for Students and Instructors

Small Group Benefits for Students

Positive group experiences have been shown to contribute to student learning, retention, and overall college success (National Survey of Student Engagement, 2006).

"One hand washes the other." "Two heads are better than one." "It takes a village." "Teamwork makes the dream work." The familiar adages speak of the potential in the benefit to all parties involved when they work together toward a common goal. If properly structured, group projects can help students develop skills that will enhance productivity, creativity, and leadership abilities for life and work. Moreover, group work promote other abilities including:

- Give and receive feedback on performance
- Break complex tasks into parts and steps
- Develop stronger communication skills.
- Plan and manage time
- Refine understanding through discussion and explanation
- Challenge assumptions
- Patience with conflict
- Problem-solving strategies
- Unbiased judgements

Group projects can also help students hone skills that are specific to collaborative efforts as well, allowing them to . . .

- Tackle more complex problems than they could on their own.
- Delegate roles and responsibilities.
- Share diverse perspectives.
- Develop their own voice and perspectives in relation to peers.
- Combine knowledge and skills.
- Hold one another (and be held) accountable.
- Develop confidence to take risks.
- Develop new approaches to resolving differences.
- Establish a shared identity with other group members.

- Find positive peers to emulate.
- Assert leadership roles and incorporate the efforts of others.
- Confidently implement innovative concepts and ideas.
- Share platforms and opportunities to advance knowledge and causes.

It is of great importance to understand that merely assigning groups can and will not guarantee successful outcomes. Groups that are successful must be designed, assessed, and supervised in ways that promote meaningful teamwork and dedicated collaborations, otherwise they will dismantle and backfire resembling utter disaster and chaos.

Small Group Benefits for Instructors

Every instructor has heard the moans and groans of students when a group assignment is given. Instructors too, have had the task of working in these same types of groups and here we are years later enforcing the same fate on others, which clearly means that it did not "kill either of us." The fact is . . . it really came in handy as it introduced many to skills, insight, and strategies they live by in dealing with work, relationships, and students, and the benefits are endless.

Instructors have the liberty to assign more complex assignments to groups that would be too overwhelming for individual students. Group work also introduces more unpredictability in teaching, since groups may approach tasks and solve problems in a more innovative and interesting ways. This can be refreshing for instructors as it is always exhilarating to witness students utilize, create, and execute effectively using knowledge and strategies taught in a subject. They may approach tasks and solve problems in novel, interesting ways. This can be refreshing for instructors. In addition, group assignments can be useful when there are a limited number of project topics to distribute among students or even when dealing with large classes. This can also aid in the reduction of the number of final projects instructors have to grade.

Instructors are to keep in mind that which supersedes whatever teaching benefit, to always assign group work task that fill the learning objectives of the course and promote collaborations. And that group work can also have with it its own grading difficulties, as all who are assigned to groups do not participate fully or not at all and grading nightmares can certainly arise.

COMM 1003: Fundamental of Speech Communication

Group Speech Rubric		
Group Member	Date _____	Class Section_____
Group Member		
Group Member		
Group Member		
Group Member		
TOPIC:	Speech Time _____	Score_____/150

Legend S: Superior	E: Excellent	G: Good	A: Average	I: Poor	M: Missing

Presentation Content

	M	I	A	G	E	S
Organized	0	6	7	8	9	10
Attention Getter	0	6	7	8	9	10
Preview of Main Points in Intro 1. 2. 3.	0	6	7	8	9	10
Clear 3 Main Points	0	6	7	8	9	10
Supporting Material (3 sources heard) 1. 2. 3.	0	6	7	8	9	10
Transitions	0	6	7	8	9	10
Summary & Review of Main Points	0	6	7	8	9	10
Total _____ / 70						

Delivery/Professional Appearance

Group Cohesion	0	6	7	8	9	10
Verbal Communication	0	6	7	8	9	10
Nonverbal Communication, professional attire	0	6	7	8	9	10
Total _____ / 30						

Presentation Aids

Integrated/Enhanced Presentation	0	6	7	8	9	10
Total _____ / 10						

Outline

Typed & Formatted	0	6	7	8	9	10
Spelling/Grammar	0	6	7	8	9	10
1 source per body point (3 total) and Reference Page	0	6	7	8	9	10
Well Developed Arguments	0	6	7	8	9	10
Total _____ / 40						

Comments

_____

_____

Member 1 _____

_____

_____

_____

Member 2 _____

_____

_____

_____

Member 3 _____

_____

_____

_____

Member 4 _____

_____

_____

_____

Member 5 _____

_____

_____

_____

PART 4

How Public Speaking is Used

Chapter 10

Teach Me Something—Speaking to Inform

Learning Objectives

Exploration in this chapter will allow students to discover:
10.1 Defining Informative Speaking and How It Differs from Persuasive Speech
10.2 Identify Common Topic Categories for Informative Speeches
10.3 Strategies for Effective Informative Speaking
10.4 Strategies for Orally Citing Sources
10.5 Introductions, Transitions, Conclusions and Informative Speech Rubric

© Albert H. Teich/Shutterstock.com

Want to possess the power to grant inspiration, wealth, and knowledge? . . . Dare to be informative.

— Author's own

Scenario

Taylor was meeting in the library with her friend's sisters Imani and Sanaa to discuss their upcoming informative speech assignment given by their professor in class earlier in the week. She was anxious because she had no idea what she was going to talk about and the speech topic approval was the next day. Hopefully she and her friends could brainstorm and figure something out that would be interesting enough for the entire class. Taylor entered the library and spotted Imani and Sanaa at a center table with notepads and their open textbook. "I'm glad you guys remembered your textbooks, I am crazy nervous about this speech and selecting an appropriate topic. I see you both already have a page

© michaeljung/Shutterstock.com

full of notes so it appears that I am in the right place. Imani will you please give me some insight on selecting topics?"

"Sure I will," responded Imani with a reassuring smile. "These notes we have are the brainstorming lists of topics and the cognitive maps Professor Cameron talked about during lecture the other day in class. It seemed like a lot when he drew the examples on the board but it's a really useful method for narrowing great topics." "Remembering also, to start with topic's that are of interest to you or affect you personally somehow has helped us decide on the topic that we are going to present for approval tomorrow," Sanaa added.

"Well, I'm feeling better already, I'll start my brainstorming list now, in the meantime what topics did you guys come up with?" asked Taylor. "Well I!" said both sister's simultaneously. The three having a good laugh, Imani began, "we are what you call "army brats" and both our parents were enlisted and stationed in Belgium when I was born then later we were stationed here in the states, thus making me a duel citizen, so I decided to do my informative speech on 'Dual Citizenship'."

"Our family was stationed at Fort Hood near Killeen, Texas, and on November 5 the day our mother gave birth to our younger sister there was a mass shooting, considered the worst ever on a military installation. Our mother had to be rushed from recovery so that the wounded could be treated, so my informative speech is going to be about "mass shootings on military installations," Sanaa enthusiastically stated.

"You two have really chosen some great topics that are going to be of great interest to the audience, especially because of your credibility. I even want to hear more but I'll wait until actual speech day like everyone else," Taylor laughed. "Oh by the way, the cognitive map really worked girls, my mother is a recording artist and I love singing as well and had the opportunity to record my first song on a Christmas album with my mother, so my informative speech will share the process of recoding music."

"Great!" Imani yelled. "Professor Cameron will be happy to know we used the strategies he taught us, we will be ready with solid topics in tomorrow's class, our work here is done, . . . movie anyone?"

The students in this scenario represent a common situation for many students preparing for the informative speech process, selection of topics can be complicated if the right strategies are not utilized. As you read this chapter think of other characteristics of informative speaking that would assist Taylor, Imani, and Sanaa in selecting appropriate topics.

10.1 Defining Informative Speaking

As you'll recall from Chapter 3, "The Speech and How It All Comes Together," speaking to inform is one of the three possible general purposes for public speaking. The goal of informative speaking is to teach an audience something using objective factual information about objects, people, events, processes, concepts, and issues. Interestingly, informative speaking is a newcomer in the world of public speaking theorizing and instruction, which began thousands of years ago with the ancient Greeks. Earlier in the text we spoke of the ancient Greek philosophers Aristotle, Cicero, and Quintilian who believed that public speaking was rhetoric, which inherently served only to persuade listeners and was not based on factual data. Public speaking was argumentative and a matter of debate even for teaching purposes.

To what do we owe gratitude for this change in public speaking history? Society . . . because information is not jealously protected by guilds or individuals as it once was, now it is believed that information should be shared and available to the masses. Important to know is how informative speech differs from persuasive speech, below we will address these differences.

- *Speaker's motivation*: A significant difference between informative and persuasive speeches addresses the speaker's motivation. The motivation of informative speakers is to impart knowledge, or new information about a subject matter to their audience. This is achieved by providing facts, stats, and general evidence while making clear understanding during the process of teaching. Informational speeches do not tell people what to do with the information; their goal is for the audience to have and understand the information.
  Supporting evidence: The second difference between informative and persuasive speeches is how supporting evidence is used. We learned earlier in the text that supporting material is to add interest and prove, which is done by definitions, illustrations, statistics, and comparisons. The more evidence an informative speaker can provide for their audience, the more options they have to make informed decisions.
- *Speaker expectation*: The third difference between informative and persuasive speeches is the speaker's expectation of their audience members. The difference between the two lies in the speaker's end goal and what the speaker wants the audience to leave with. Effective informative speakers want the audience to be impacted by the content and leave with full understanding of the topic concepts. In contrast, persuasive speakers know that their audience will not be completely vested in their content or message from hearing just one speech, so it may take several attempts to change the opinions, values, or beliefs of individuals, as persuasion most often occurs over a period of time.

10.2 Identify Common Topic Categories of Informative Speeches

Being a successful informative speaker starts with choosing a topic that can engage and educate the audience. Your topic choices may be influenced by the level at which you are speaking. Informative speaking usually happens at one of three levels: formal, vocational, and impromptu (Verderber, 1994).

- **Formal**: Formal informative speeches occur when an audience has assembled specifically to hear what you have to say. Being invited to speak to a group during a professional meeting, a civic gathering, or a celebration gala brings with it high expectations. Only people who have accomplished or achieved much are asked to serve as keynote speakers, and they usually speak about these experiences.
- **Vocational:** Professors like the author spend many hours lecturing, which is a common form of vocational informative speaking. In addition, compliance officers give informative presentations on sexual harassment policies while human resource managers do the same type of presentations concerning company policies, rules, and regulations to new employees.

- **Impromptu:** We are all subject to impromptu informative speaking as we convey information during our daily interactions whether it's giving a student directions to the registrar office or the student center, summarizing an episode of Law and Order to a friend who missed it, or bringing someone up to speed on a breaking news report on CNN are all examples of impromptu informative speaking on a daily basis.

Whether at the formal, vocational, or impromptu level, informative speeches can emerge from a range of categories, which (as stated above in our definition of informative speaking) include objects, people, events, processes, concepts, and issues. An extended speech at the formal level may include subject matter from several of these categories, while a speech at the vocational level may convey detailed information about a process, concept, or issue relevant to a specific career.

To assist students in the speech selection process, a graph is presented in Figure 10.1 as a navigation system of the range of categories following an explanation to each.

Speeches about *objects* convey information about any nonhuman material things. Mechanical objects, animals, plants, and fictional objects are all suitable topics of investigation. Strive to choose one of which your audience is less familiar with or shed light on a familiar one with new findings and interesting facts.

Speeches about *people* focus on real or fictional individuals who are living or dead. These speeches require in-depth biographical research; an encyclopedia entry is not sufficient. Introduce a new person to the audience or share little-known or surprising information about a person we already know.

Speeches about *concepts* are less concrete than speeches about objects or people, as they focus on notions, ideas, beliefs, theories, attitudes, and/or principles. A concept can be familiar to us, like equality, sustainable energy, or "love at first sight." When speaking about concepts, you may have to find concrete ideas in order to make abstract ideas more relatable and tangible to your audience.

Speeches about *events* then, describes the occurrence in full: the time, date, location, and circumstances of that occurrence. A particular day in history, an annual observation, or a seldom occurring event can each serve as interesting informative topics. Avoid rehashing commonly known information.

Speeches about a *process* describe how something is made, done, or work. Processes provide a step-by-step account of a procedure or natural occurrence. Speakers may walk an audience through, or demonstrate, a series of actions that take place to complete a procedure such as how to bake a cake from scratch.

Speeches about *issues* provide objective and balanced information about a disputed subject or a matter of concern for society. It is important that speakers view themselves as objective reporters rather than commentators to avoid tipping the balance of the speech from informative to persuasive. Rather than advocating for a particular position, the speaker should seek to teach or raise the awareness of the audience.

Figure 10.1 Sample informative speech topics by category

Categories	Examples	Other Examples
Objects	Video Games	Cars, Real Estate, Electronics, Aircrafts, Gold
People	Barak Obama,	George Carlin, Oprah, Etta James, Bill Clinton
Concepts	Sustainability	Mind Exploit, equality, Online trading
Events	Harlem Renaissance	Diwali Festival, Earth Day, Zydeco Festival Sundance Film Fest, Cinco de Mayo, Elections Reproduction, Growth, Voting, Scrapbooking
Processes	Converting wind to energy	Quilting, Web design, Branding & Marketing
Issues	Mental Health	Age & LGBT Discrimination, Unemployment

10.3 Strategies for Effective Informative Speaking

There are several challenges when preparing an informative speech; speakers have to be mindful to avoid persuasion, information overload, and have the ability to engage their audience.

Avoid Persuasion

For informative speaking, a speaker's purpose should be to create understanding by sharing objective, factual information. Specific purpose and thesis statements help establish a speaker's goal and purpose and can serve as useful reference points to keep a speech on track. Information should function to clarify and explain in an informative speech, the goal should not be to influence the thoughts or behaviors of audience members.

Information Overload

It is a flaw of many informative speakers to attempt to cram excessive amounts of content in a 10-minute speech. This practice is risky and will result in information overload, which is a barrier for effective listening, which occurs when speeches contain more information than an audience can hold. For that reason speakers should certainly hone their editing skills to shave off excess fat in a speech. It is as easy as the edits one makes to an email before pressing send or the letter of interest you've prepared, you are careful to say only what is necessary. Take the same into consideration when preparing your informative speech; your goal is that your audience "take away" not "run away" after your speech. Know what information is best to keep and what is best to throw away. Being a cautious editor is useful in avoiding information overload. Readers can read and reread literature if they choose but an audience member cannot conduct an independent review while listening to a speaker live.

"Give the audience words of necessity, dare not burden them with words unnecessarily."

— Author's own

Engage Your Audience

It is common knowledge that all speakers compete with internal and external stimuli for their audience' attention. Getting an audience engaged and keeping their attention throughout the presentation is a challenge for most speakers, especially when speaking to inform. Audience members are more likely to stay engaged with a speaker they view as credible. Complementing good supporting material with a practiced and fluent delivery increases credibility and audience engagement. In addition, as we discussed earlier, good informative speakers are users of objective and factual information. Repackaging information into concrete familiar examples is also a strategy for making your speech more engaging.

10.4 Basic Guidelines for Orally Citing Sources in Speeches

The many times an instructor has had to deduct points when a student does not orally cite sources during a speech is immeasurable. It is an issue of epic proportions and the author feels it necessary to provide insight and vivid examples to curtail the feelings of "my hair is on fire" every instructor feels when students exhibit such lapses.

Sources are not just to be included in the written outline, especially not in a public speaking class; we need them written and cited orally. Your perfecting your writing skills is appreciated and necessary, however, not as much here as in your English Composition classes. This is Public "SPEAKING," our main focus is your ability to speak, abiding by the rules of public speaking. Citing sources during a presentation enhances your credibility as a speaker, indicates preparedness and knowledge of your topic. Also, you are more apt to persuade an audience when they are aware that evidence supports an argument (Reynolds & Reynolds, 2002).

Citing sources in a speech has a special name. You have written a few research papers by now and have heard of a Work Cited page, Reference page, or parenthetical citations. Well "speeches" have similar citations called *oral citations*, which is a verbal reference given to a source or portion of research in a speech. Let's briefly explore what should be included during citation. Consider the following citation examples based on guidelines suggested in online articles by the College of Southern Nevada*:
What should an oral citation include?

AUTHOR

Mention the author's name, along with credentials to establish that author as a credible source.

Example:

In the March 27th, 2011 issue of the New York Times, Pulitzer Prize winning author and foreign affairs columnist Thomas Friedman wrote . . .

TITLE

Say the title of a book, magazine, journal, or website. You should identify the type of publication and provide a comment regarding credibility if the publication is not widely recognized.

Example:

In the November 10th, 2006 issue of *Practice Nurse*, the leading peer-reviewed journal for primary care nurses, author Sue Lyon describes shingles as . . .

"Titles of articles do not necessarily have to be mentioned, unless you are using several articles from the same source."

DATE

Say the date that a book, journal, magazine, or newspaper was published. If you are using information from an interview, give the date when the person was interviewed.

If you are using information from a website that doesn't clearly show a date on the document, say the date that the web page was last updated and/or the date you accessed the website.

Example:

The web page titled "The History of Figs," dated 2011, provided by the California Fig Advisory Board, reveals varied uses of the fig: as a digestive aid, a treatment for skin pigmentation diseases, and a coffee substitute.

You can use key words to develop the phrasing necessary for oral citations, such as:

- According to
- Explains
- Says (goes on to say)
- As reported by (or CNN reports that)
- Morrison writes that

The author has used CNN and Morrison as example; however, you may use what is needed for your individual research.

---

*http://libguides.csn.edu/oral-citation

10.5 Speech Introductions, Transitions, and Conclusions

Introductions

The introduction is a brief yet highly important part of any speech; it should be well planned out as its purpose is to prepare an audience to listen to a speaker's thoughts, ideas, and concepts in the body of a speech. It also serves to determine if the audience will perceive a speaker as having credibility and being someone worth listening to.

Introductions give speakers but a short time to:
- Capture and audience's attention.
- Provide the audience with relevance.
- Establish credibility.
- Clarify a solid central idea with thesis and preview of main points.

Let's explore each of these functions in detail.

Important to remember is that when you accomplish one of the four functions, you can also accomplish others at the same time. For example, when a speaker shares a personal story, it can serve to capture the attention of each one in the audience, establish credibility, and suggest the importance of your topic all at the same time.

Capture Audience Attention

Your goal here is to allow the first words you utter in your introduction gain the favorable attention for your topic, which is the attention-getter. However, speakers who open their speech with the announcement of their topic are not considered effective attention-getters. "My speech is about" . . . or "Today I am going to discuss" . . . has committed "audience shut down." No one is going to sit up in their seat with anticipation of what you're going to say next! You have accomplished losing most of your audience (except your parents or spouse who are praying for you) in just a few words of boredom.

© Click49/Shutterstock.com

Avoid the following in a speech:
- I'm nervous
- Apologies or excuses
- My name is . . . and my speech is on . . . (You and your topic have already been introduced by the instructor or host)
- Everybody is staring at me (were they supposed to leave their eyes at home?)
- Can I start over? (Your audience will want to get over "you"!)
- Um Ok
- Using "In conclusion"
- Saying "Thank you" at the end of a speech
- Asking "Are there any questions?" (the event may not allow for Q&A)

However, use these more appropriate ways of gaining favorable attention toward your topic and creating an effective attention-getter:

- Questions, actual or rhetorical (which provokes thought in listeners).
- Eye-opening statement (Love the sound of your babies cry in the morning, because every parent is not so fortunate, each year 44 percent of infants die from Sudden Infant Death Syndrome according to the Center for Disease Control.)
- Narrative, factual or hypothetical (A great story of fact or something that could happen)
- Memorable quote
- Humor (jokes or funny remark, be sure it is in good taste, relates to topic, audience-centered, and if self-deprecating avoid this without the skill to do so, it could shatter credibility)

Provide Audience with Relevance

Speakers should always strive to select a topic that is relevant to their audience. This can be accomplished by choosing a topic that is timely and current. Another approach to making a topic relevant is to tell your audience why they should listen to or be interested in the topic; this aids in promoting relevance as well. If a speaker is able to create relevance to their audience, it will increase the likelihood of them remembering the content in the speech. Relevance should be of recent information, a speech made by John F. Kennedy would not be relevant today as our society and the state of our nation have changed. Informative speeches should reflect our contemporary period, the most recent research.

Establish Credibility

The goal of every speaker should be to acquire their audience's attention and respect. Credibility to an audience is of the upmost importance, it asks questions of a speaker that if proved sufficient will ensure a speaker as an authority on their topic. Questions are as such: What do you know about the topic? What makes you an authority on the topic? Why are you interested in the subject? You may very well have answered these questions and established your credibility as part of your attention-getter. In the event that is not the case then it is appropriate to interject a statement after your attention–getter, like the following:

- I recall during my travels to Cambodia as a Reach Out Volunteer, building houses on the school grounds for the village of Siem Reap. Where the local teenagers eagerly gathered to assist and give back to their communities.

If by chance you will be introduced to the audience by someone else, be sure to include information that speaks of your credentials and experience as related to your topic in a short biography you have provided prior to the event.

Clarify a Solid Central Idea with Thesis and Preview of Main Point

This is the final purpose of your introduction. It is also the foundation of your speech and usually comes at the end of the introduction, without a well-constructed central idea with a thesis and preview of your main points a speech has no bases and will fall apart. Many times speakers do well with stating relevance and credibility but fail at make their central idea and position clear. This frequent mistake causes an audience to become confused and distracted from active listening. Ending your introduction with a good thesis statement and preview not only makes your purpose and main points clear, it serves as an effective transition into the body of your speech.

Recall in Chapter 3, that a central idea and thesis preview can be accomplished in a single sentence or two for the sake of clarity. The following is an example of two sentences that will accomplish your goals:

- Reach Out Volunteers travel abroad changing the lives of many underserved countries. To truly understand reach out volunteers it is important to know who they are, what countries they serve, and how you too can become a volunteer.

Speech Transitions

Another element in planning your speech is transitions, which serve to help you move from one main point in your body to another. Speech transitions are magical words and phrases that help your argument flow smoothly. They often consist of a single transition word or a short transition phrase, but occasionally form an entire sentence. In a written speech, speech transitions are generally found at the start of paragraphs.

© iQoncept/Shutterstock.com

Transitions should be planned ahead and added to your outline otherwise they will be typical poor announcements of your next main point such as "First," "Next," "Secondly," or "Lastly." Quite elementary! Little thought has gone into the transitions at all and is indicative of a novice speaker. The author dares to challenge you, even the novice has to be creative and scholarly when adding transitions to your speech and outline, you may even forget you are a novice, your audience sure may.

Transition examples:

- Volunteering is an honor. You may have dreamed of international adventures, now let's explore how those dreams can become a reality.
- Now that you understand the abusive backgrounds many teen mom come from, let's look into how to strengthen our culture on personal responsibility regarding sex.

  Transitions are important in written form, in research papers and essays, but are even more important in a speech. It is important to note that if readers get lost or need clarity, they can always go back and reread material. Listeners, however, do not have the convenience of relistening to a live speech.

Instructors challenge students to write at least five transitions as a brief exercise on the perforated sheet below. Create a thesis statement of your choice (or students can create their own), write it on the board and let students have about 10 minutes to do the exercise.

Figure 10.2 Transition Practice Sheet

	Transition Practice Sheet
1	
2	
3	
4	
5	

Speech Conclusions

The very last part of your speech is the conclusion. Your introduction creates an important first impression and credibility, the conclusion is equally important in creating a lasting impression. The conclusion serves two functions: to summarize your main points (a restatement or your thesis and preview) and provide a memorable closure to your speech.

Summarize Main Points

The summary is a reminder to your audience of the central idea and the main points you covered earlier in the introduction of your speech. Also, it is the last chance the speaker has to be sure listeners remember the content and will take away information that speaker provided. Be mindful when concluding not to say "In conclusion"; a well-constructed conclusion will make it evident to your audience that you are ending your speech without calling attention to the mechanics of your speech. Below are a few examples of summary statements:

- After learning what BASE jumping is, looking at how it got started, and a little bit of what is going on today, you can determine if you want to be one of the official elite BASE jumpers or just continue jumping off your roof into the pool instead.
- Now that you know the abusive background many teen parents come from, and how to strengthen our culture on personal responsibility, you can make an informed choice about being a mentor at the national campaign to prevent teen pregnancy.

Memorable Closing

You have many ways in which to arrive at your memorable closing.

Here are some interesting choices:
- Close with a story—You then tell a brief story with a moral, and then tell the audience what the moral is. Don't leave it to them to figure out for themselves. Often you can close with a story that illustrates your key points and then clearly links to the key message that you are making with your speech.
- End with laughter—You can close with humor. You can tell a joke that loops back into your subject and repeats the lesson or main point you are making with a story that makes everyone laugh.
- Poetic ending—You can close with a poem. There are many fine poems that contain messages that summarize the key points you want to make. You can select a poem that is moving, dramatic, or emotional. Perhaps even write your own short piece.
- Close with inspiration—You can end a speech with something inspirational as well.
  If you have given an uplifting talk, remember that hope is, and has always been, the main religion of mankind. People love to be motivated and inspired to be or do something different and better in the future.
- Close memorable quote—Use a quote from a widely recognized and respected person. It should be brief, one to three sentences, worded in a particularly memorable way that ties into the main points in the body. Don't shy away from quotes that injects humor or a flair for the dramatic.

Never use the conclusion to introduce new ideas, do not end abruptly and leave audience without closure, and never end with the words "The End," "That's a Wrap," "That's all I have." The ultimate goal in a closing is to be memorable using dramatics, humor, cleverness, insight, and power. And no matter how tempting it may be, Never Ever "Drop the Mic!"

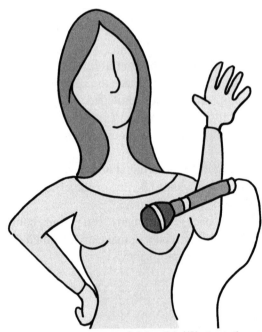

© John t Takai/Shutterstock.com

****** PLEASE BRING THIS FORM ON YOUR SPEECH DAY ******

COMM 1003: Fundamental of Speech Communication

Informative Speech Rubric	
Group Member	
Date _____	**Class Section**_____
TOPIC:	**Speech Time** _____ **Score**_____ / 200

Legend S: Superior   E: Excellent   G: Good   A: Average   I: Poor   M:Missing

Presentation Content

	M	I	A	G	E	S
Organized	0	6	7	8	9	10
Attention Getter	0	6	7	8	9	10
Preview of Main Points in Intro 1. 2. 3.	0	6	7	8	9	10
Clear 3 Main Points	0	6	7	8	9	10
Supporting Material (3 sources heard) 1. 2. 3.	0	6	7	8	9	10
Transitions	0	6	7	8	9	10
Summary & Review of Main Points	0	6	7	8	9	10
Final Thought	0	6	7	8	9	10
Total _____ / 80						

Delivery/Professional Appearance

Extemporaneous, Proper Use of Notecards	0	6	7	8	9	10
Eye Contact	0	6	7	8	9	10
Nonverbal Communication, Professional Attire	0	6	7	8	9	10

Voice; Vocal variety, fillers etc.	0	6	7	8	9	10
Gestures x 6	0	6	7	8	9	10
Movement; Posture, shifty-foot, V-stance,	0	6	7	8	9	10
Total _____ / 60						

Presentation Aids

Integrated/Enhanced Presentation	0	6	7	8	9	10
Well Designed and organized	0	6	7	8	9	10
Total _____ / 20						

Outline

Typed & Formatted	0	6	7	8	9	10
Spelling/Grammar	0	6	7	8	9	10
1 source per body point (3 total) and Reference Page	0	6	7	8	9	10
Well Developed Arguments	0	6	7	8	9	10
Total _____ / 40						

Comments

_____

_____

_____

_____

_____

_____

_____

_____

_____

_____

Chapter 11

All We Do Is Argue—Speaking To Persuade

Learning Objectives

Exploration in this chapter will allow students to discover:
11.1 The Foundation of Persuasion, How Persuasive Speeches Differ from Informative Speeches
11.2 Strategies for Choosing Persuasive Speech Topics
11.3 Aristotle's Primary Means of Persuasion
11.4 Persuasive Organizational Patterns
11.5 Persuasive Speech Rubric

© Everett Collection/Shutterstock.com

"Persuasion is the civilized substitute for harsh authority and ruthless force." R.T. Oliver

"I have read over this speech three times and am uncertain what else it needs to appeal to the Volunteer Coalition campus chapter to sign petitions banning these new food sharing laws being put in place." Dupree tossed his notes on the table, folded his arms and looked over at his partner Duke shaking his head. "It's of great importance to garner as much support as we can to advocate for and be the voice of the homeless in our community."

"We have great proof of the church and community organizations in other cities that have be penalized and shut down for feeding the homeless; we have illustrations as well as interesting facts that will relate to the students, but will it be interesting enough get them to volunteer and help us? That's what we need—their help," Duke agreed.

Scenario

© Uber Images/Shutterstock.com

"You're right the presentation has all those things but something is missing. I am concerned that it won't be persuasive enough. We are not even sure that students have ever heard of the National Coalition for the Homeless and may not understand how much nonprofit organizations depend on volunteers, we can't pay them to do this," Dupree replied.

Duke stood up with his hands in his pockets. "You're right." Interesting facts alone won't be enough. We have to make them care enough to want to become volunteers."

"You don't think the facts will persuade them?" Dupree asked. "That's all it took for me when I heard about the number of faith-based organizations who had to close their soup kitchens and turn away hungry women and children, it persuaded me enough to take action."

"I think it would be safe to say that it was more than just the numbers that persuaded you," Duke suggested. I think it was the fact that women and children were involved and you had the thought of a small child having to go to bed hungry. I believe you had an emotional response to the facts you heard."

"Perhaps you are right." Dupree conceded. "But will that be the same for this audience?" Most college students are not parents with children."

"Maybe not. . ., but college students today were once children; many of whom may have experienced watching a parent struggle to make ends meet, perhaps one paycheck away from being homeless themselves. Poverty doesn't discriminate Dupree, appeal to them with that in mind and I believe you will have a powerful persuasive presentation," Duke passionately expressed.

"Wow!" Dupree gushed. "I should let you give this speech, your insight moved me. It is just the approach I will take; it is great that the Student Volunteer Coalition invited me to speak at their next event, now I am more confident that we will accomplish our goals acquiring new student volunteers in banning food sharing laws in our community."

Dupree and Duke in our opening scenario realize that their approach is important the first time because persuasive speeches unlike informative speeches usually take several times to get people to change their minds. As we learn about persuasive speaking in this chapter, make note of ways you too can improve on your approach to persuading others.

11.1 Foundation of Persuasion and Differences between Persuasive and Informative Speeches

We produce and receive persuasive messages daily, but we don't often stop to think about how we make the arguments we do or the quality of the arguments that we receive. In this section, we'll learn the foundation of persuasion and how it differs from informative, how to choose a good persuasive speech topic, Aristotle's primary approach to persuasion, and how to prepare an audience-centered persuasive speech along with the basic guidelines for citing sources during a speech.

Foundation of Persuasion

Persuasive speaking seeks to influence the beliefs, attitudes, values, or behaviors of audience members. In order to persuade, a speaker has to construct arguments that appeal to audience members. We are bombarded by multiple persuasive messages every day from people you are familiar with: radio, television, billboards (now digitally designed ones), internet, and even on your mobile devices. Important to your understanding is: learning how to listen critically to persuasive messages to recognize and avoid manipulation. It is equally important to understand how to craft persuasive messages to be able to effectively influence others on the basis of credibility and ethics. Aristotle, a Greek philosopher, said: "Persuasion is achieved by the speaker's personal character when the speech is so spoken as to make us think him credible."

Difference between Persuasive and Informative Speeches

One way to get clarity of something is to contrast it with something else, as we did in Chapter 10 with the contrast of informative speeches with persuasive speech; and the same goes here, we will contrast persuasive and informative here in brief detail.

- *Speaker's motivation*: The motivation of informative speakers is to impart knowledge or new information about a subject matter to their audience by providing facts, stats, and general evidence. Persuasive speakers' motivation on the other hand is to present information in order to change the way the audience thinks or acts by using logical, ethical, and emotional appeals.
- *Supporting evidence*: In informative speeches the more evidence a speaker can provide for their audience the more options they have to make informed decisions, which is done by definitions, illustrations, statistics, and comparisons. Whereas persuasive speakers use supporting information to prove that only certain beliefs or actions are acceptable.
- *Speaker expectation*: Informative speakers want the audience to be impacted by the content and leave with full understanding of topic concepts. In contrast, persuasive speakers know that their audience will not be completely vested in their content or message from hearing just one speech; it may take several attempts to change the opinions, values, or beliefs of individuals, as persuasion most often occurs over a period of time.

To get as much change in attitude as possible, it is imperative that speakers analyze their audience carefully to know which arguments are likely to be the most successful.

Without this knowledge as summarized in Figure 11.1, speakers' chances of being persuasive are severely diminished.

Figure 11.1 Analysis of Audience's Values, Beliefs, Attitudes, and Behaviors.

A speaker's chance of successfully persuading an audience is affected by whether they choose to target the audience's attitudes, behaviors, beliefs, and values. Attitudes are at the surface of the model because they are easier to change than beliefs or one's core values. Beliefs can be changed but not as easily as attitude and behaviors. Values are at the lower level of the model as they are most deeply ingrained and are met with the utmost difficulty to change.

11.2 Strategies for Choosing Persuasive Speech Topics

Good persuasive speech topics are current, controversial, and have important implications for society. If your topic is currently being discussed on television, in newspapers, in the lounges in your dorm, or around your family's dinner table, then it's a current topic. A persuasive speech aimed at getting audience members to have car insurance would not be a topic that would have much current relevance, given that statistics show that most people already have car insurance, this would have been relevant in the late 1970s and early 1980s.

Many topics that are current are also controversial, which is what gets them attention by the media and ordinary citizens. Current and controversial topics will be more engaging for your audience. For instance, Americans needing medical insurance is neither current nor controversial; however, the matter of Americans having mandatory health insurance imposed upon them is controversial. If they do not purchase coverage, a fine is assessed for themselves, their spouse and each of their tax dependents is both relevant and controversial and would be considered a suitable persuasive speech topic.

Also, look for topics that are important to you and to society as a whole. Power and conviction are bound in the words in which we speak; it is through communication that we participate in something and become change agents. Therefore, every opportunity to address an audience should be to taken seriously with topics of substance. Choosing a speech topic that has implications for society is probably a better application of your public speaking skills than choosing to persuade the audience that the Dallas Cowboys are better than the Houston Texans or if the video game Call of Duty Black Opts 3 is better than Battlefield. Although, the topics may be of interest to you, they do not carry the same social weight as other topics you could have chosen to speak about.

Choose topics that merge with your own interests and passions. If you are biology major, it would make more sense to do a persuasive speech on funding for advanced medical research rather than on capital punishment. If certain topics are triggers or hot buttons for you, avoid those in an academic or professional setting, as this could hinder an ethical and audience-centered delivery not to mention diminish any hopes of your audience viewing you as a speaker with credibility.

You also want to ensure that your topic is actually persuasive. Draft your thesis statement as an "I believe" statement so your stance on an issue is clear. Also, think of your main points as reasons to support your thesis. Students end up with speeches that aren't very persuasive in nature if they don't think of their main points as reasons. Identifying arguments that counter your thesis is also a good exercise to help ensure your topic is persuasive. If you can clearly and easily identify a competing thesis statement and supporting reasons, then your topic and approach are arguable.

Choosing a Persuasive Speech Topic Review

Choose a topic that is current
- **Not current:** People should have car insurance.
- **Current:** People should attend the National Museum of African American History and Culture.

Choose a topic that is controversial
- **Not controversial.** People should have health coverage.
- **Controversial.** Should Americans pay when they can't afford health coverage.

Choose a topic that meaningfully impacts society
- **Not as impactful.** Call of Duty Black Opts 3 is better than Battlefield.
- **Impactful.** Police officers should be assigned to communities that best suit their frame of reference.

Write a thesis statement that is clearly argumentative and states your stance
- **Unclear thesis.** Teacher/Student relationships have become common in the United States.
- **Clear, argumentative thesis with stance.** A teacher–student relationship violates student trust and degrades an honored and respected profession. Therefore, it is important that stricter monitoring policies be enforced, age limits requirements to teach certain grade levels and harsher jail sentences be mandated.

11.3 Aristotle's Primary Means of Persuasion

According to Aristotle there are three primary "means of persuasion" aka types of persuasive appeals: ethos, logos, and pathos.

Ethos

Ethos refers to the credibility of a speaker and includes three dimensions: competence, trustworthiness, and dynamism. The two most researched dimensions of credibility are competence and trustworthiness (Stiff and Mongeau, 2003).

© Dean Drobot/Shutterstock.com

- *Competence*—refers to the perception of a speaker's expertise in relation to the topic being discussed. The audience is more apt to listen if you have a certain level of expertise, which is the first step toward being persuaded.
- *Trustworthiness*—a person of good character who the audience perceives as a speaker that provides accurate credible information without manipulation. They are mindful to enhance their speech with solid research by orally citing the sources of content. Competent speakers know the content of their speeches and are also able to deliver it effectively.
- *Dynamism*—the degree to which an audience perceive a speaker to be outgoing, approachable, likable, and enthusiastic. There are in fact two components to dynamism and they are charisma and energy.

- Charisma—abstract and concrete qualities that make a speaker attractive to an audience and cause people to be drawn to them. Charismatic people know that they possess such traits as they have been told this at some point in their lives and attracting others is a norm for them. Unfortunately, charisma is a "you either have it or you don't" kind of thing, some people have a naturally charismatic personality and others do not. One would have great difficulty trying to intentionally develop such a characteristic.
- Energy—is something anyone can tap into, having enthusiasm for your topic, using eye contact, well-used vocal variety, and perhaps engaging slide shows can increase your dynamism.

Logos (Reasoning or Logic)

Speakers employ logos by presenting credible information as supporting material and verbally citing their sources during their speech. Choosing material that is verifiable and unbiased can also appeal to logos, as well as citing personal experience. Moreover, presenting a rational and logical argument is important, but speakers can be more effective persuaders if they bring in and refute counterarguments. The most effective persuasive messages are those that present two sides of an argument and refute the opposing side, followed by single argument messages, followed by messages that present counterarguments but do not refute them (Stiff and Mongeau, 2003).

Pathos (Emotional Appeal)

Stirring emotions in an audience is a way to get them involved in the speech, and involvement can create more opportunities for persuasion and action. It will also cause the audience to feel personally connected to your topic and position. The ability to use vocal variety, cadence, and repetition to rouse an audience's emotion is not easily attained. Think of how stirring Martin Luther King Jr.'s "I Have a Dream" speech was due to his ability to evoke the emotions of the audience. Dr. King used powerful and creative language in conjunction with his vocalics to deliver one of the most famous speeches in our history. There are many ways to move a person emotionally:

© LifetimeStock/Shutterstock.com

- Visual images
- Stories
- Guest testimonies
- Use of vivid language to paint word pictures for audience members
- Vocal variety, cadence, and repetition

Speakers should strive to appeal to ethos, logos, and pathos within a speech. A speech built primarily on ethos might lead an audience to think that a speaker is full of himself or herself, completely self-centered. A speech full of facts and statistics appealing to logos would result in information overload as spoken about in Chapter 10. Speakers who rely primarily on appeals to pathos may be seen as overly passionate, biased, or unable to see others' viewpoints; this could also make one's audience extremely uncomfortable.

11.4 Organizational Patterns for Persuasive Speech

Earlier in the text in Chapter 3, we discussed how to organize a speech; however, there are specific modes of organization that are unique to persuasive speeches. The way your persuasive speech is organized will determine how effective it will be. Many instructors will often assign the organizational pattern they prefer students use for the persuasive speech, but students might like to choose the one they favor. We will briefly discuss several in this section.

1. Problem–solution: This is a method for analyzing and speaking about a topic by identifying a problem and proposing one or more solutions. This format involves argumentation where the speaker wants the audience to take a particular course of action, and speaker will also persuade listener on the causes as well.

2. Problem–Problem–Solution: This is a method for presenting a two-part problem and proposing a one-part solution. The format involves argumentation; speaker wants the audience to take a particular course of action.

3. Refutation: This is described as the negation of an argument, opinion, testimony, doctrine, or theory, through contradicting evidence. It normally constitutes a part of the speech that disproves the opposing arguments.

4. Cause and Effect: Cause is why an event or action takes place. The effect is an event that takes place due to the cause. Speakers will first present the cause of the problem to the audience; what follows is the speaker must now reveal how the problem directly affects the audience.

5. Motivated sequence: Designed by Alan Monroe in 1930. Monroe's Motivated Sequence is an organizational pattern designed for persuasive speaking that appeals to audience members' needs and motivates them to action. Speeches with call to actions would benefit greatly by using this organizational pattern with examples in italics:

   • **Attention**: Grab the audience attention by making the topic relevant to them.

   Imagine being on an exotic international vacation unfamiliar with many of the customs and you become ill and have to be hospitalized and they will not honor your medical coverage. Your bill is insurmountable for your three-night stay. Because you cannot pay, you have been denied departure. This issue has occurred with many Americans abroad and should garner national attention and resolutions.

   • **Need**: Cite evidence that the issue should be addressed.

   The US Embassy or consulate has been notified of the ongoing issue. Americans should check their medical benefits before traveling abroad to see what it will cover overseas. If your coverage provides services outside the United States remember to carry both of your identification cards or purchase international medical coverage with your travel agent.

   • **Solution**: Offer audience a solution and ensure them that it is well thought out.

   Contact the American Citizens Service Unit at the US Embassy or Consulate; they can assist in locating appropriate medical services and notifying family and friends. If necessary, a consular officer can also assist in the transfer of funds from the United States.

   • **Visualization**: Take your audience beyond your solution, allow them to visualize the improved situation if your plan is adapted.

   International travel should be an exciting and memorable adventure. Becoming ill or injured away from home is scary and sometimes part of those memories. But if we are proactive in knowing our benefit coverage allowances and purchasing international coverage with travel agents, your experience abroad should be more rewarding.

   • **Action**: Call your listeners to action by providing concrete steps to follow.

   I urge you to take action by first making your friends and family aware of this issue. Second, notify your medical coverage provider, and register with the US Embassy before traveling, also know the laws that govern that country's medical emergency policy concerning American citizens. I have brought brochures with insurance travel tips with questions you need to ask as well as information where you can reach the US Embassy. Please take one at the end of my speech, a bit of information will make a huge difference.

****** **PLEASE BRING THIS FORM ON YOUR SPEECH DAY** ******

COMM 1003: Fundamental of Speech Communication

Persuasive Speech Rubric	
Name	
Date _____	**Class Section**_____
TOPIC:	**Speech Time** _____	**Score**_____ / 200

Legend S: Superior   E: Excellent   G: Good   A: Average   I: Poor   M: Missing

Presentation Content

	M	I	A	G	E	S
Organized	0	6	7	8	9	10
Attention Getter	0	6	7	8	9	10
Thesis and Preview of Main Points in Intro 1. 2. 3.	0	6	7	8	9	10
Clear 3 Main Points	0	6	7	8	9	10
Supporting Material (3 sources heard) 1. 2. 3.	0	6	7	8	9	10
Transitions	0	6	7	8	9	10
Summary & Review of Main Points	0	6	7	8	9	10
Final Thought	0	6	7	8	9	10
Total _____ / 80						

Delivery/Professional Appearance						
Extemporaneous/ Proper Use of Notecards	0	6	7	8	9	10
Eye Contact	0	6	7	8	9	10
Nonverbal Communication, Professional Attire	0	6	7	8	9	10
Voice	0	6	7	8	9	10
Gestures x 6	0	6	7	8	9	10
Movement- Posture/Oratory Triangle	0	6	7	8	9	10
Total _____ / 60						

Call to Action					
Organized	3	3.5	4	4.5	5
Well Designed	3	3.5	4	4.5	5
Used Appropriately	3	3.5	4	4.5	5
Enhanced Speech	3	3.5	4	4.5	5
Total _____ / 20					

Outline					
Typed , Complete Sentences & Formatted	0	6	7	8	9	10
Spelling/Grammar	0	6	7	8	9	10
1 source per body point (3 total) and Reference Page	0	6	7	8	9	10
Well Developed Arguments	0	6	7	8	9	10
Total _____ / 40						

Core Curriculum Assessment				
Invention/Organization/drafting/revision/editing	1	2	3	4
Audience & Purpose Appropriate	1	2	3	4
Applies Modes of Expression	1	2	3	4
Understands the Communication Process and Audience Analysis	1	2	3	4
Well Developed Arguments	1	2	3	4
Demonstrates the ability to give oral presentations	1	2	3	4

Comments

_____

_____

_____

_____

_____

_____

Chapter 12

Being Career Ready

Effective Communication in the Interviewing Context

Learning Objectives

Exploration in this chapter will allow students to discover:

12.1 Different Types of Interviews—What Constitutes a Quality interview?

12.2 Informational Interviews and Their Benefits.

12.3 Panel Interviews,—What Are the Interviewer and Interviewee Responsibilities during interview?
Be Smart . . . Look the Part: Dress for Success

© Pressmaster/Shutterstock.com

"Now sir, you know exactly why I'm here; I gotta eat, gotta be in doors, gotta drive, and gotta wife. Now this here piece of paper took me four years to git says I'm qualified. Now won'tcha let me come on back out here tomorrow and show ya."

— Authors own

12.1 Different Types of Interviews

If you have this text you are more than likely enrolled in an institution of higher learning, which is a strong indication that you are working toward obtaining a degree in your area of interest, and securing a promising offer from a Fortune 500. Therefore, interviewing is going to be of great importance to you now or in the near future. We have mentioned several times in the text about communication as it relates to you in the workplace, now we will discuss in detail some much needed insight into the interviewing process. Several types of interviews to possibly prepare for have been discussed in the following.

Types of Interviews

Interview is a somewhat formal discussion between a hirer and an applicant or candidate, typically in person, in which information is exchanged, with the intention of determining the applicant's suitability for a position. These usually happen between two parties but traditional processes of interviewing have evolved as such that interviewing concepts have changed.

Panel interviews: A panel interview is one that is conducted by a group of interviewers. This has become standard practice in corporate America. Sometimes you will meet with the interviewers separately, and other times you will meet with them as a group (panel). Sometimes there will even be multiple candidates interviewing at the same time. Typically, each interviewer will ask you at least one question.

Presentation interviews: Some interviews will challenge you with a business issue and ask you to present solutions to one or more situations. You may be given 15 minutes to prepare and 15 minutes or less to present. The key here is to put pen to paper immediately to get thinking fast. In the first five minutes or less, outline the problem and as many solutions that come to mind in words. Drawing diagrams or pictures may help, too. Next, circle the solutions you think are the best or the ones for which you have the most ideas on how to implement. After that, brainstorm what resources you need to apply to each solution in under five minutes (Yeager, 2014).

Also, this type of interview could require you to present research that proves you are qualified for the position, and may very well be in a panel-type setting.

Performance interviews (aka performance evaluations): These are used by businesses and nonprofit organizations as a way to assess and encourage quality performances and goal setting of employees at all levels or the organization. Promotions, rewards, discipline, and even terminations may be tied to these performance reviews.

Persuasive interviews: Used by sales personnel, marketing specialist, or fund-raisers as a new way to sell a product, change an attitude, or collect money.

Exit interview: When an employee leaves the company for any reason, an exit interview is conducted. Aims at eliciting information about the job or related matters, and help the employer in having a better insight into what is right or wrong about the company.

What Constitutes a Quality Interview?

Being that this is going to be one of the most important forms of communication for you, it is valuable that you know what constitutes a quality interview.

- **Do your research**
  This is required of both interviewer and interviewee. The candidate should have background knowledge of the company for which he is applying as well as the person or persons interviewing them. The interviewer should be familiar with the candidate's resume and cover letter, also before the interview Google the person to see if anything interesting comes up. Also, check to see if they have a Facebook, Twitter, or Instagram profile, what type of content and activities appear on those profiles.

- **Questions**
  Asking and answering questions are a skill set in and of itself and is very necessary for a quality interview. Both parties are asking and answering questions seeking to obtain information.
- **Planning**
  An interview doesn't happen on a moment's notice, they take time to happen; quality interviews require prior thought and careful planning by both parties. This entails the actual searching for the company in which to apply, updating your resume to submit to the company, and going through the painstaking time-consuming online application process.
  You now need to prepare to communicate to someone of whom you are fortunate to know that can review your application; an interview will be scheduled allowing enough time for you to research, practice asking and answering questions, as well as picking out the appropriate power suit.

If you implement the above-mentioned tips, you will be well prepared for a quality interview.

12.2 Informational Interviews and Their Benefits

An informative Interview is a one-on-one conversation with someone who has a job you might like, who works within an industry you might want to enter, or who is employed by a specific company that you're interested in learning about. These interviews are excellent options for plotting a career path or focusing your aspirations. "It's a way to learn more about what a day is like in the field, you get inside perspectives before you jump in" (Crawford, 2012). This is also referred to as networking, and you do this by asking these types of questions that should only take about 15 minutes and a minimum of five to six questions:

- What is a typical work day like?
- How is the corporate culture?
- What is the management style?
- What are corporate trends?
- What type of resume is required?
- What is the typical salary range for employees?
- What forms of questions are usually asked during interviews?

The informational interview is best suited for the new job seeker, and anyone planning a career change and persons seeking a promotion. You should be mindful to start with your inner circle of family and friends who may have leads on your area of interest, keep in mind this is to acquire information, not to land a job. This method is to make sure you build rapports so that people will know you and possibly refer you. Also, when you make these informational interview appointments, send the questions ahead of time to indicate that you are prepared. Be professional and always adhere to the time slot you have been granted as these professionals have busy agendas.

Benefits of Informational Interviews

Consider some key benefits of informational interviews suggested in an online article by Michigan State University, which are as follows.

Learning: If you want to find out what a specific career path has to offer, what the positives and negatives are within an organization's culture, or which academic major will best prepare you for a selected career path, why not ask the people who are already working within that field?

Building relationships: In a recent national survey, 70 percent of respondents reported they got their present position because of a personal contact. The earlier you start building relationships with people in your field of interest, the stronger they will be when you actually begin your job hunt later on.

Linking: See how your skill development, courses, and academic planning can connect to your future success on the job.

12.3 Responsibility of Interviewer

Good interviewers do two things. They:

- plan questions to elicit the best possible comments
- perform the interview so it sounds smooth and polished

Planning Questions

Questions are the tools the interviewer uses to get the information from interviewee.
  The right questions have to be asked whether you are conducting an employment interview or an informational interview.
Well-phrased questions will direct their thoughts and encourage them to address the specific issues you need them to talk about.
Planning questions is both an art and a science. They need to both open the topic up as well as stimulate a response. Questions may be 10 words or as few as one. Often a well-expressed "really" with a raised eyebrow can get a more interesting response than "do you really think that everyone has the same opinion?"
Good interviewers prepare their questions in advance when they do their resume, cover letter, background research, and work. However, they often generate new ones in response to discussion that takes place during the interview.

Performing Questions

Planning questions that are well-phrased and evoke the right response are only half of the equation.
  Asking *open-ended questions* will allow for more in-depth, richer, more detailed information. These questions are broad and allow applicants to adopt various approaches. Applicant responses can be time consuming but your goal is to get the desired information needed to acquire the most suitable candidate.
Follow-up Questions: These are useful in eliciting narratives or stories from applicants and they relax the applicant as well.
  Verbal and Nonverbal Probes—verbal probes are:
  "really?", "Interesting," or "Tell me more." Nonverbal probes are: leaning forward in chair, direct eye contact, and smiling.
Avoid Unlawful Questions: To maintain compliance with the Equal Employment Opportunity Commission (EEOC.gov), these two guidelines must be followed at all time during interview questions:
  1. All questions must be job related.
  2. All applicants for a position must be asked the same basic questions.
  Applicants cannot be asked questions about things such as their religion, health, or where they are from. Moreover, there cannot be separate questions for women and men, minorities, people over 50 and the like, as everyone should be treated equally.

Interviewee Responsibility

Be prepared for different interview styles, no two interviewers' interview the same way.
Familiarize yourself with the typical mode of questions at interviews, which is called *standard questions* as they relate to applicants' basic skills and qualities. Standard questions include "Where do you see yourself in five years?" "What do you think you can bring to our organization?" "Why are you here today?" Effective interviewees will practice answers to questions beforehand to ensure that their answers

flow easily during interviews. The best interviewers will ask complex behavior questions, which appeal to the applicants' creativity and ability to cope with real-life circumstances. Interviewee does have to think deeper and demonstrate skill to answer such behavioral questions.

Overall, an interviewee must:
Be prepared
Know details about the organization and the actual position
Bring copies of resume and other needed documentation
Have questions ready to ask interviewer
Dress professionally
Arrive early

Dress For Success

Book It, Look It, and Hook It!

© Maridav/Shutterstock.com

© michaeljung/Shutterstock.com

In job-hunting, first impressions are critical. Remember, you are marketing a product—yourself—to a potential employer, and the first thing the employer sees when greeting you is your attire; thus, you must make every effort to have the proper dress for the type of job you are seeking. Will dressing properly get you the job? Of course not, but it will give you a competitive edge and a positive first impression.

Should you be judged by what you wear? Perhaps not, but the reality is, of course, you are judged. Throughout the entire job-seeking process employers use short-cuts, or rules of thumb, to save time. With cover letters, it's the opening paragraph and a quick scan of your qualifications. With resumes, it is a quick scan of your accomplishments. With the job interview, its how you're dressed that sets the tone of the interview (Hansen, 2009).

© Daniel Jedzura/Shutterstock.com

© kurhan/Shutterstock.com

Amy Glass, a trainer and coach at Brody Communications Ltd. of Jenkintown, Pennsylvania, and an expert on presentation skills, business etiquette, professional presence and interpersonal communication, states that "you want and need to have the best image possible. A conservative suit, shirt and tie if you're a man, or a conservative suit if you're a woman, with—perhaps—personality shown through your shirt or jewelry."

In industries such as advertising, public relations, graphic design and information technology, what to wear might be less clear. If that's the case, Glass says, ask about the company's general dress policies when you're first contacted about an interview.

"You can say to the person you speak with, 'I want to make sure I understand your company culture and dress appropriately'," Glass notes. "It's not a bad thing at all. In fact, it shows respect." If in doubt, err on the conservative side.

"Adorn your skills and talents as the gifts they truly are, present them proudly . . . for the unwrapping reveals offerings that will change the world."

— Authors own

Appendix

The Harlem Renaissance 1

by Sheila Teague, March 22, 2016

Can you imagine yourself as a young African American in the 1920's being emotionally oppressed by a systematic racism for years and your only way of mental freedom was through self-expression? Neither Can I. But according to Langston Hughes in one of his famous poems "Mother to Son" that was the harsh reality.

Although African Americans encountered violent racism at that time, African Americans still found a way to overcome their sorrow. The Harlem Renaissance was a way for African Americans to express themselves in ways that they never could before. Moving from the South to the North also known at that time as the Great Migration, African Americans found a new way to not only express themselves but, it allowed them to create a new positive image of African Americans as a whole.

The Harlem Renaissance brought forth great African American art and literature such as the journal "Fire" or classic poems from the legendary Langston Hughes such as "Mother to Son" and "As I grew older" The Harlem Renaissance was a movement of African American art, literature and music.

Let's look at how the Harlem Renaissance movement began. Dealing with harsh laws and racism imposed specifically on African Americans, African Americans gathered their family and their belongings and migrated North. There they found that the North gave them opportunity both economically and socially. It was during the Great Migration that African Americans would find a new sense of freedom. This new sense of discovered freedom allowed them to build and reshape the image of African Americans in an artistic and positive ways sparking the beginning of the Harlem Renaissance.

Though African Americans found their new sense of freedom and self-pride they still battled with the daily struggle of racism. Instead of African Americans letting the daily struggle of racism effect their movement, they turned something negative into something positive. In the book "Harlem Renaissance" by Nathan Irvin Huggins, he explained how despite the difficult times African Americans still believed that they could spark a "rebirth in their community." These Harlemites were so convinced that they were evoking their people "Dusk of Dawn" that they believed they marked a Renaissance.

So now that you know about the beginnings of the Harlem Renaissance, we can discuss the writers and the activists that helped spark the movement. Well known writer and political activist W.E.B du Bois had many theories on how to gain rights for African Americans. He believed in a theory called the "talented tenth" a certain group of African American intellectuals would help educate and gain rights for the race as a whole. During the time of the Harlem Renaissance Du Bois wrote a series of books that would uplift and educate the African American Community. Books such as the "Souls of Black Folk" and the "Dusk of Dawn" would become very popular at that time.

The Book "Black Folk Then and Now" sheds light on one of Du Bois colleagues William Ferris, on how gifted W.E.B du Bois was in literature and as a leader. "He is one of the few writers who leaped in front as a leader and became the head of a popular movement" (Moses, Intro). Langston Hughes another well-known writer and poet also expressed his views on the injustice towards African Americans. One of Hughes many poems "Oppression" paints a picture of how someone back then could lose his or her ability to "dream" for better days. Both W.E.B. Du Bois and Langston Hughes played a major role behind the Harlem Renaissance. Both creatively found ways to express their views through literature adding on to the Self Pride that continued to flourish in the African American community at the time.

Throughout the early 1920's the Harlem Renaissance continued to leave an impact on the African American community. The impact would help outsiders to understand the culture and the harsh realities African Americans faced. Many of the artist and writers such as James Weldon Johnson and Langston Hughes would give that insight to the daily struggles of African American life both elegantly and creatively.

The Book "The Harlem Renaissance in Black and White" by George Hutchison explains some of the specific things that the Renaissance impacted. "The cultural movement known as the "Negro Renaissance" depended on a general congruence of economic expansion and re enlighten among the ruling elites" which in returned encouraged the transformation in the fields of art, literature, and cultural critique. (Hutchison,4)

You can see that the Harlem Renaissance definitely made an impact on the view of African Americans at that time. So When you hear the words "Life for me aint no crystal stair" don't just think of Langston Hughes, think of James Weldon Johnson, think of W.E.B. du Bois, think of Zora Neale Hurston, think of Booker T Washington. Think of all who lived during that time whose lives weren't so easy to make sure that you can live a better one.

Being a Child of Immigrant Parents 2

By Naomi Deneke March 22, 2016

My family is from a country where, in their youth, education was given to the privileged and few. My grandparents had schooling until grade school, and soon had to drop out to help their families in their home country, Ethiopia. My mother and father were one of the first to receive higher level education in their families, but soon experienced hardships due to political and religious civil war in Ethiopia. This lead to their decision to move to America. They came to the US when my mother was nine months pregnant with my older brother, and just a year and a half later gave birth to my twin sister and me. My father worked three jobs while attending Howard University, and my mother worked two jobs while taking care of me, my sister, and brother. There are many sacrifices that immigrant parents make, and in turn they have many expectations. This comes with being a child of immigrant parents or as I call it a first generation kid.

There are many families with similar situations, and it is important to acknowledge and recognize them. Therefore children can relate to one another and understand the significance of being a first generation kid. As the daughter of parents who migrated from Ethiopia, I understand what it is like to be raised in America by foreign parents.

Being a child of immigrant parents carries responsibilities and expectations beyond what the average American kid experiences. To truly understand what being a child of immigrants is like, it is important to know the circumstances of immigration, the expectation placed on first generation children, and the opportunities America gives that other countries cannot provide.

First, we should know why so many people leave their native land. There are a number of reasons. According to a Global Citizen article, the following are some of these reasons: to escape persecution, violence or conflict, to find refuge due to environmental factors, to seek healthcare, to escape poverty, to find better opportunities for their children, and to find better job and educational opportunities (Nunez, 2014). Another contributing factor is that America is a very fair and tolerant country unlike other parts of the world where you may be persecuted for your religious, political, and social views. Perhaps due to the fact that America has historically been populated by immigrants, allowing different cultures to influence our governance. My own parents came to the states because of political and religious persecution in Ethiopia, and to provide my siblings and me with a better living environment and educational opportunities. As a student, I see numerous international students. Prairie View A&M University has about a 3% population of international students. More than often, there are a combination of reasons for why people migrate to America.

Next we should discuss what expectations are set for first generation children. Of course every family is different, but from my experience, there are some universal expectations for most. First is respect. I have an abundance of respect for my parents for the sacrifices they made on behalf of my siblings and I, and many other parents would expect the same from their children- though that is not always the case. Often times there is friction due to cultural differences. One of the hardest tasks to accomplish as a foreign parent is instilling the culture of their country into their children while in a completely different country. If your parents came to the US to provide you with better opportunities (like mine did), then you are probably expected to go to college. Education is probably the biggest factor when it comes to "expectations" and, according to the Sociology of Education Journal, there are often discrepancies between what parents and children deem as sufficient or an achievement (Hao, 175). Success is not always defined the same for a first generation child as it is for an immigrant parent (i.e. becoming a doctor, lawyer, or engineer).

However, getting the opportunity to become a doctor, lawyer, or engineer can be difficult in other countries. So many families come to America because they know there are many services provided here that are not in their home country. According to Tomasevski, the average age a child stops receiving education worldwide is between the ages 6-12 (2006). In America you have the opportunity and resources to succeed even though you may fail, but in other countries you have very few or no opportunities or resources. Thus, making it almost impossible to succeed. In some countries, citizens are not given the right of our first amendment freedoms (religion, speech, press, protest, and petition). American healthcare is considerably better than most other countries, and we have the most basic amenities like electricity, running water, and toilets that some families did not have access to in other countries. These are all things we must remember not to take for granted. As a first generation child, our parents remind us of the privileges we are granted today.

As you can see, being the child of immigrant parents can be different and interesting. Parents immigrate for many different reasons, and that can affect the expectations placed on their children, but what is most important is getting better opportunities. One thing I can say as a child of two immigrant parents is that I really value every opportunity I have been given. Especially my education because I know how hard it is for young African-American girls like myself to get a decent education in other parts of the world. Hopefully, I can make a change to supply more people with the opportunities I have been given.

Diwali "Festival of Lights" 3

by Gokul Babudas March, 24, 2016

I know everybody here has heard the slang "it's lit". It has a lot of different meanings but Diwali literally means it's lit, everything and anything is decorated with colorful lights.

Diwali is the "festival of lights' it signifies the victory of good over evil, light over darkness and knowledge over ignorance. It marks the Hindu New year and it is celebrated by over 1.2 billion people, of which an estimated two million people celebrate Diwali in the United States. (Barooah) I've celebrated Diwali my entire life and it is one of my favorite festivals, and I want to share with you why I like it so much. Diwali is celebrated all around the world and has gotten very popular in recent years due to social media. To truly understand Diwali, it's important to look at the history of it, how it is celebrated in India and how Diwali celebrations continue today.

First, let's look at the history of Diwali. There are a lot of mythical and historical reasons behind the Diwali celebrations. The most well-known story behind Diwali is in the Ramayana, Rama the prince of Ayodha was ordered to go away from the country and live in the forest for fourteen years. To celebrate the prince's homecoming, the people of Ayodhya lit their houses with earthen lamps and decorated the entire city in the grandest manner. Diwali is celebrated on the 15th day of the month of Kartika on the Hindu calendar, which falls between the middle of October and middle of November. It is celebrated by four different religions- Hinduism, Sikhism, Jainism, and Buddhism. Diwali has a very rich history, now that we know a bit of it; let's look at how it is celebrated in India.

Each year people of all communities celebrate this festival to welcome a new ray of hope into their lives through this festival, when all the negative forces are believed to be removed from both, one's home and life. Diwali is a five day festival of lights. Houses are decorated with earthen candles and locals decorate their houses with colorful rangoli artwork-patterns created on the floor using colored rice or powder. During Diwali, families and friends share sweets, gifts, and there is also a strong belief in giving food and goods to the less fortunate. The main foods that are associated with Diwali are Indian sweets, which come in a range of colors and flavors. Wearing new clothes is also part of the tradition, as well as the tradition of gambling.

Certain Diwali traditions vary from place to place in India; together we will explore what some of them are. The celebration of Diwali has been modernized in the recent era. The earthen candles have been replaced by colorful lighting bulbs. Fireworks have been incorporated into the celebration and in addition to sweets, bhang is also a popular Diwali item. Bhang is an edible preparation of cannabis, typically used in lassi which is a popular traditional yogurt-based drink from the Indian Subcontinent and originates from the Punjab. Fireworks are burnt by children and people of all ages during the night to celebrate the occasion. Devotees go to temple and dance; the form of dancing is called Garba, and devotees dance around the gods.

The festival of lights transcends religion and is unanimously celebrated by Indians worldwide all over India with great zeal. For Diwali festival, people do shopping of cloths and gold ornaments, which they wear before goddess Laxmi pujan. People get the blessing of Lord Ganesh and Goddess Laxmi in the form of health, wealth, prosperity and happiness.

Flowers, sweets, food, amongst others are some of the ways in which people try to start a fresh and welcome a new year of bliss. Hopefully you have a better understanding of what Diwali is, after learning about its history, how it was celebrated in India and how it continues to be celebrated today, perhaps you can determine if it is a festival you should partake in. I would like to leave you with a quote in Hindi "PREM KA EK DEEPAK PRAKAASH" Which translates as "light a lamp of love".

Spirited Driving 4

By Bryston Roberts March 24, 2016

Imagine being behind the wheel of a two door coupe, pushing your vehicle to its limits through the twist and turns of a hilly country road. You are smiling and laughing as the g-forces push you deep into your seat. No, you're not trying to get a speeding ticket, and no you're not trying to test the laws of physics; you're just having a good time.

From flying down the Interstate, to peeling off at stop lights, I'm sure at least a few of you have had the urge to bury your right foot deep into the carpet to see what your vehicle could do. Although some of you may not be comfortable with the idea of pushing your car to its limits, I constantly have to remind myself that I have to respect the laws of the road. Because I do find great joy in spirited driving, I have decided to take this time to inform you guys on a pass time that is very near and dear to my heart.

Spirited driving has become a favorite past-time for many Americans, and to truly understand spirited driving, we need to know what it is, the difference between spirited driving and reckless driving, and where it happens. First let's take a look at what spirited driving is.

For those of you who don't know, spirited driving is pure fun! Spirited driving is an exciting method of operating a motor vehicle; taking a car to its performance limits. In order to engage in spirited driving, you have to have the right mindset. Safe spirited driving is not something that you can just command to happen. You really have to focus and know not only your limits, but the limits of the vehicle that you are driving. You should really strive to become one with their vehicle when you push it to its limits. However, spirited driving is so much more than speeding down open road, it can be just about anywhere your car will allow you go.

For those of you who thought that spirited driving is just for the road, you are sadly mistaken. Many people take their vehicles to the limit off road. Whether it's racing and jumping over the sand dunes in Baja, taking their jeeps and other four-by-fours slowly while rock crawling up mountains, or rally racing. Rally racing is really cool because it features street cars with modified suspensions and very sophisticated all-wheel drive systems to help them handle not only paved roads at high speeds, but the usually unpaved and unforgiving road courses in the mountains and plains.

So spirited driving can happen just about anywhere, have any of you guys thought about ice drifting? Although spirited driving can be fun in any form, when it comes to spirited driving it is important to know the difference between reckless driving and spirited driving.

For most people after a long stressful day at work there's only one thing that they want to do, and that's to go for a drive. However, down the highway when you get off work wouldn't be the best time to drive with too much enthusiasm. There may be traffic out; your visibility could be impaired by a number of factors. That's why it's important to be safe and to make sure that you know the difference between safe and stupid.

Reckless is when you are endangering the lives of others. If you're on an empty road or a closed course be as spirited as you want! But when you're not, please obey all traffic laws and warning signs. Just because your car can go two hundred miles per hour, doesn't mean that it should. Know your limits. It's important to think about not only your safety, but the safety of those who you might be sharing the road with. Remember these roads are public, people will not only be driving on them, but working on them, and walking across them.

It is my hope that you have a better understanding of what spirited driving is now. After learning what it is, you should now know that it can be dangerous. But at the same time it can be one of the small joys in life that make life worth living. For many people like me they can't help but to live life a quarter mile at a time. And in the words of the late Paul Walker, "If one day the speed kills me, don't cry, because I was smiling." Be safe everyone, and have fun.

CPSIA information can be obtained
at www.ICGtesting.com
Printed in the USA
LVOW02s1408220417
531779LV00002B/4/P

9 781524 911232